MW00604976

Emerging *from* Darkness

MOSAICA PRESS

Emerging *from* Darkness

CHANUKAH

RABBI AHRON RAPPS

ISBN: 978-1-952370-15-1

Published by Mosaica Press, Inc.
www.mosaicapress.com
info@mosaicapress.com

לזכר נשמת
שר ואלוף בישראל

הרה"ג רב ישראל יחזקאל בן רב יואל
פלוטשאק זצ"ל

ראש ישיבת דרך חיים
אב למשפחתו ולאלפי תלמידיו
הדריכם בנועם והטעימם מצוף דבש תורת ה'
ת.נ.צ.ב.ה.

הונצח ע"י משפחתו

לזכר נשמת

ר' זאב בן ר' יהושע
חיה הינדא בת ר' אהרן הלוי
ראפס

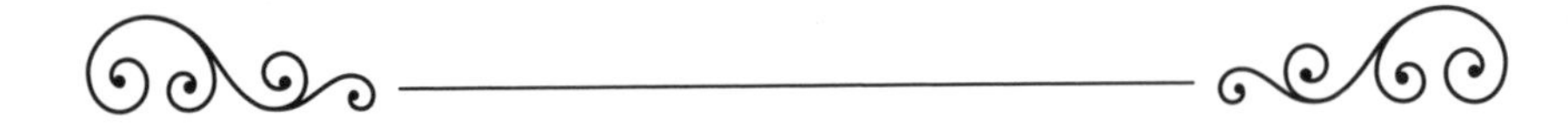

לעילוי נשמת

Reb Mendel Beer ז"ל

בעל חסד נפלא

Who was truly מחשיב תורה ולומדיה

ת.נ.צ.ב.ה.

MRS. BRACHA BEER AND THE RAPPS,
KOBRE, AND BEER FAMILIES

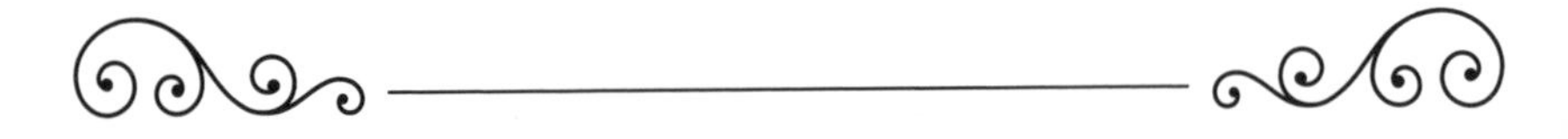

Mesivta Yeshiva Rabbi Chaim Berlin

מתיבתא רבנו חיים ברלין

MESIVTA HIGH SCHOOL ORACH CHAIM

RABBI SHLOMO BRAUNSTEIN
Menahel
RABBI MICHEL GUZIK
S"Gan Menahel
RABBI YOSEF LANDSBERG
Principal, General Studies

כ' אב תש"פ

מרן הרה"ג רב יצחק הוטנר זצ"ל בעל הפחד יצחק השריש בתלמידיו ובכל מי ששתה בצמא את דבריו במאמריו ועצותיו שיהיו שונאים את שטחיות בהבנת התורה

ובפרט בעניני השקפה ומה שקוראין היום עניני מחשבה שכל עיקר תכלית הלימוד בענינים אלו הוא להכניס את האדם לפנימיותה של הלכות דעות וחובות הלבבות שהן בעצם דברים סתומים ועמוקים מן השטח הפשוט

הרב אהרן ראפס שליט"א עוד מנעוריו הכיר את אמיתת הגישה הנ"ל בדברי תורה ועשה את עצמו כמבקש בכל כוחו להבין את העמקות הטמונה במאמרי הפחד יצחק ובביאורי הראשי הישיבה הרה"ג הרב אהרן שכטר שליט"א והרה"ג הרב יונתן דייוויד שליט"א ותלמידיהם הרמ"ים והאברכים שניתגעו הרבה בהבנת תורת מרן זצ"ל

ורב אהרן בתשוקה גדולה ובלי ביישנות היה שואל ודורש ביאורים עמוקים ופנימים מכל תלמיד חכם שהיה לו שייכות לפנימיות הענינים עד שקיבל וחקר ודרש וקנה לעצמו רכוש גדול בענינים העומדים ברומו של עולם ובעומק הבנתם

והנה במשך הימים שהיה רב אהרן שליט"א תלמיד בהישיבה הגדולה דסטאמפורד זכה להתקרבות להרה"ג הרב משה שפירא זצ"ל ונעשה כאחד מתלמידיו המובהקים והלך וגדל עד שכמעט כל ענין שעסק בו מצא בו מרגניתא , חידוש עמוק הראוי לדפוס וזכה לפרסם פניניו וחידושיו שבוע בשבוע בהעתון היתד נאמן ובהרבה שיחות שהגיד לכל מבקשי תורתו ובשנים האחרונות באופן קבוע למבוגרי תלמידי ישיבת רבינו חיים ברלין וכולל גור אריה

ולכן שמחנו לשמוע שרב אהרן שליט"א ליקט ותיקן הרבה משיעוריו שנאמרו ונדפסו באופנים שונים וקבצם וסדרם לדפוס להוציאם לאור בספר חשוב מאוד ויהי רצון שיתקבל הספר בשתי ידים בעולם התורה ובהישיבות לראשי הישיבות ותלמידהם , ומובטחני שספר זה ודבריו העמוקים המאירים וברורים יביאו הנאה גדולה לכל המבקש דברי תורה שאינם שטחים ורגילים

הכו"ח באהבה רבה ובברכת הצלחה רבה

שלמה בראונשטיין
מנהל מתיבתא רבנו חיים ברלין

מכבר הכרתי מעשיו של המנהל רב שלמה להמשך עיניו בבוגרי הישיבה במעלותם ועליתם, ובהנאה משתף אני דברי לדבריו על מעלת המחבר רב אהרן ראפס שליט"א

אהרן שכטר

הרב ראובן נירענבערג
ר"מ בישיבת רבינו חיים ברלין

כ"א אב תש"פ

לכבוד תלמידי הנעלה והאהוב הרה"ג הרב אהרן ראפס שליט"א,

אשריך שזכית לצקת מים על ידיהם של גדולי בעלי מחשבה שבדורינו,

אשריך שזכית להבין עמקי סודותיהם,

אשריך שאתה זוכה להוציא פרי עבודתיך בלשון קל ובהיר לשותים בצמא דבריך,

יהי"ר שיתקבלו ברצון.

הכו"ח לכבוד התורה ולומדיה
ראובן נירענבערג

הרב אברהם דוב הלוי ברומברג, ראש הישיבה
הרב מנחם מינק, ראש המתיבתא

טז׳ תמוז תשפ׳

בספר נחלת יעקב לרבינו הנתיבות פרשת בהעלותך כתב להקשות למה לא מצינו איש מתנבא בימי משה מלבד אהרן עד שאמר לו הקב״ה אספה לי שבעים איש ואפילו יהושע לא היה מתנבא, ואחר מיתת משה בימי הנביאים היו נביאים לרוב כדמבואר בקרא (שמואל א׳ י-י) והנה חבל נביאים לקראתו , והאיך דורו של משה אשר לא היה שום דורות כמותן עד שהקב״ה אמר מי יתן והיה לבבם זה כל הימים (דברים ה-כו) לא יהיו מוכנים לנבואה כדורות אחרונים

וכתב לתרץ דכמו שהשמש מכהה אורות הכוכבים עד שאינם נראים כלל כמו״כ מעלת משה היה גדולה מאוד והיה מכהה אור כל הצדיקים נגד השי״ת ולא היה מדבר רק עם משה כי פני משה כפני חמה משא״כ יהושע ושאר נביאים אשר היו כפני לבנה שאין אורה גדול כ״כ נראין ג״כ אורות הכוכבים וכמו״כ נראו אור שאר הצדיקים אחר מיתת משה וזהו שאמרו אוי לאותה בושה כי אין בושה גדולה מזו במה שלא נחשבנו נגד משה לכלום

ולכאורה קשה א״כ למה אמר הקב״ה אספה לי שבעים זקנים , ולמה אין משה מכהה אור השבעים זקנים ? ונראה משום דכתיב ואצלתי מן הרוח אשר עליך ושמתי עליהם דלא היה נבואתן אלא מן הרוח אשר על משה ואז גם נבואתן מאירה

רבינו הגדול הגאון ר׳ משה שפירא זצ״ל היה כפני החמה ואורות החכמים העומדים למולו לא היו נחשבים כנגדו והיו כלא היו, ידידי הרה״ג ר׳ אהרן ראפס שליט״א היה מבואי בית מדרשו והיה מסתופף בצלו ונאצל מן הרוח אשר על פני רבינו משה וגם חכמתו מאירה ואפריון נמטי לידידי הרה״ג הנ״ל שאסף וביאר יסודות רבותינו זצ״ל להעתיקם בלשון אינגליש כדי ששאר העם יוכל להבינם וקורא אני עליו חכם גדול אתה (נגעים ט-ג) ״שקיימת דברי חכמים״

אברהם דוב בה״ר יונה הלוי ברומברג

הנני לכבוד התורה ולומדי׳
אברהם דוב בהר״ר יונה הלוי ברומברג

ADDRESS 1951 New Central Ave. Lakewood, NJ 08701 MAILING ADDRESS P.O.B. 451 Howell, NJ 08701
PHONE 732.942.3900 FAX 732.942.3901 EMAIL office@yshnj.org

פינחס דוד הלוי הורוויץ
בלאאמו"ר כ"ק הרה"צ מוהר"ם זצוקללה"ה
מבאסטאן

בס"ד

הנה ידידי היקר והמצוין הרב אהרן ראפס שליט"א עומד להוציא לאור עולם ספר חשוב מעניני השקפה והוא תמצית של שיעורים שהשמיע לתלמידים מקשיבים במשך תקופה ארוכה

והרבה משיעורים אלו השמיע לתלמידים מקשיבים בבית מדרשנו ויכולני להעיד שהרבה מהמקשיבים הרגישו תועלת גדול בדבריו היקרים

ואני תפלה שיפוצו מעינותיו חוצה וחפץ השם בידו יצליח להמשיך בעבודת הקודש הצלחה מרובה להגדיל תורה ולהאדירה

כעתירת המברכו בכל לב

פינחס דוד הלוי הורוויץ
בלאאמו"ר הרה"ק מבאסטאן זי"ע

Rabbi Pinchas D. Horowitz / 2822 Avenue J / Brooklyn, N.Y. 11210

הרב יחיאל מיכל שטרן

רב ומו"צ בשכונת עזרת תורה

בס"ד

כ"ב תמוז תש"פ

לעונג הוא לי לראות את עבודה הרבה שעשה ידיד נפשי ה"ה הרב הגאון רבי אהרן ראפס שליט"א בספרו על ענייני המחשבה.

הרה"ג הנ"ל כולו מחשבה ובכל דבר מביט בעומק הענין, ומיוחד הוא בבקיאותו בספרי המהר"ל ועוד.

הנ"ל מעביר שיחות ומפרסם מערכות בעתוני החרדים בענינים הנ"ל.

בטוחני כי רבים יהנו לאורו.

יתן הקב"ה ויצליח להמשיך דרכו הרמה במיוחד בקירוב תלמידי הישיבה.

בידידות לנצח

יחיאל מיכל שטרן

Table of Contents

Acknowledgments

TO LEGITIMATELY THANK those who are responsible for whatever sense of virtue one possesses requires a true understanding of the meaning of what those individuals actually provided. As in all aspects of *avodah*, words could perhaps ring hollow unless they are accompanied with *kavanas ha'lev*, the true commitment of one's heart.

The Gemara in *Masechta Gitin* (60b) teaches us that "*devarim she'baal peh*"—the *chelek* of Torah that was given at Har Sinai from Hashem to Moshe Rabbeinu and serves as the Oral Law—was not permitted to be written down. The Yom Tov of Chanukah represents this *chelek* of Torah and, as such, lacks a formal *masechta*, which the Yom Tov of Purim possesses in terms of *Masechta Megillah*. Ultimately, when there was the fear of it being forgotten, it was an "*eis la'asos la'Hashem*" and was thus permitted to be written down, but in a somewhat abridged form, to retain the spiritual dimension of *Torah She'baal Peh*. Rav Tzadok, in his *sefer Resisei Laylah*, explains that the process through which the *mesorah* of *Torah She'baal Peh* is transmitted is from the *lev* of the *rebbi* to the *lev* of the *talmid*. *Peh kulmesa d'liba*, the mouth serves as the quill of the heart, and thus, it is *baal peh*—as the mouth reveals the Torah emanating from the *etzem chiyus*, the life force of the *rebbi*'s heart, to the essence and sense of being of the *talmid*. The word in the Gemara "*aliba*," which is literally translated as meaning "according to," is actually a combination of the words of *ah* and *liba*, meaning "upon the heart." For when words of Chazal were said in the Gemara, they weren't merely opinions being offered; rather, they were ideas ingrained upon the heart of the person who was speaking, and they revealed their true essence. What exists in the general sense within the *mesorah* of *Torah She'baal Peh* exists within the four walls of the *beis midrash* as well.

I, together with my whole *chaburah*, learned in Mesivta Yeshiva Rabbi Chaim Berlin and were *zocheh* to be *to'em* from just such a *matzav*. The *hadrachah* of the yeshiva was established by the Rosh Hayeshiva, *zt"l*, Maran Harav Yitzchok Hutner, *zt"l*, *Baal Pachad Yitzchok*, and thus, the relationships that we were *zocheh* to acquire were for life. In a sense, that was appropriate, for it was life itself that we were being *mekabel* from the yeshiva in terms of *limud haTorah* as well as how to live a life of Torah. We therefore recognize the need to acknowledge and say **"Thank you!"**

To the Roshei Hayeshiva, **Harav Aharon Shechter**, *shlita*, and **Harav Yonason David,** *shlita*

To the *rebbeim*, **Harav Chaim Kitevitz**, *shlita*, and **Harav Yosef Fruchthandler**, *shlita*, who gave from their *etzem chiyus*, their Torah that was "*aliba*," to inspire and develop us into becoming the *bnei Torah* we were ultimately able to become. The *pasuk* in *Parashas Va'eschanan* (6:7) says, "*V'shinantam l'vanecha*—You should teach thoroughly to your children." Chazal in the *Sifri* reveal that the word "*l'vanecha*," to your children, refers to one's *talmidim*. For us, the yeshiva served as the *makom* where these words of Chazal were realized.

To **Harav Reuven Nierenberg**, *shlita*, who introduced me to these *inyanim* and fostered in me a lifelong connection to the flavor of the *divrei Torah* contained in this *sefer*.

I would also like to acknowledge my profound and overwhelming indebtedness to Harav Moshe Shapiro, *zt"l*, as I was also *zocheh* to be his *talmid* and to receive the benefits of his caring *hadrachah* in the *limud* of these *inyanim* and his willingness to discuss and elucidate them as well.

To **Harav Zev Ha'kohein Hoberman**, *zt"l*, **Harav Gershon Weinrib**, *zt"l*, and **Harav Zevulun Schwartzman**, *shlita*, who all gave of their priceless time to learn with me and were all a source of wise counsel.

To **Harav Moshe Plutchok**, *shlita*, the Rosh Yeshiva of Yeshiva Derech Chaim and *rav* of Kahal Shaarey Torah, who served as the catalyst that brought this *sefer* to fruition. I consider him a true friend, and I value our relationship immensely. Together with the Rosh Kollel, **Rav Akiva Eisenstadt**, we have been *zocheh* to be *marbitz Torah* in Yeshiva Zichron Shraga and the Manhattan Beach Community Kollel.

I would also like to express my sincere appreciation and gratitude to:

Rav Pinchos Lipshutz, publisher and editor of the *Yated Ne'eman*, for his friendship and for allowing me to serve as his partner in being *marbitz Torah* through the written word on the *parashah* and in "Insights" all these many years.

Mesivta Yeshiva Rabbi Chaim Berlin, for giving me the opportunity to be *marbitz Torah* through saying *shiurim* to the alumni of the yeshiva. Specifically, to Rav Avrohom Fruchthandler, for enabling this to occur.

Rabbi Doron Kornbluth and the rest of the staff of Mosaica Press, who, from the start, were a pleasure to work with and supplied the expertise and guidance necessary for such a project to succeed.

Words cannot suffice to thank my parents, **Mr. and Mrs. William Rapps**, *a"h*, and in-laws—my father-in-law, **Reb Mendel Beer**, *z"l*, and my mother-in-law, *shetichyeh*, who were always there for us and continue to help us in countless ways.

And to **my wife**, who has always been an *eizer*, providing support and assistance, and who has played a major role in the publication of this *sefer*. May Hashem grant us much *nachas* from our children and grandchildren.

Ahron Rapps
Tammuz 5780

Introduction

THE PROCESS THROUGH which a person seeks a life of *kedushah* and closeness to Hashem in the midst of the evil that permeates our world is truly something remarkable. We live in a world of darkness, and we desperately seek some way to emerge from that sorry state—to one of *ohr*, the spiritual light of the connection to Hashem. This development represents the essence of living a Jewish life, and to that end, the first mitzvah that the Torah commands us is "*Ha'chodesh ha'zeh lachem*...—This month [Nissan] shall be for you the beginning of the months, it shall be for you the first of the months of the year."[1] With these words, Hashem commanded us with the mitzvah of *Kiddush Levanah*, the sanctification of the moon, where we are told to acknowledge that each month, the moon itself emerges from its own sense of darkness to reflect the light of the sun once again. The plight of the moon serves to mirror Man's *avodah* while on this world.

In *Bereishis*, we learn, "And G-d made *ha'meoros ha'gedolim*, the two great luminaries, the greater luminary to rule by day and the lesser luminary to rule the night."[2] Chazal reveal that the reason why the moon became the lesser body of light was because it complained that there cannot be two kings who serve equally with one crown. Hashem therefore told it to go and lessen itself. This represents the moon's process of decreasing in size from the fifteenth of the month until

1 *Shemos* 12:2.

2 *Bereishis* 1:16.

it becomes invisible at the end of the month to be reborn once again through the new moon. Theoretically, this process can occur because the moon is not a source of light but rather merely reflects the light of the sun. During the course of the month, because of the changes in the way in which the sun casts its light upon the moon, the moon reflects different amounts of light accordingly. In order for the moon to always appear full, either it would have to bear and project its own light, or it would somehow exist within a process of reflecting all of the sun's light. Rabbeinu Bachya on this *pasuk* in *Bereishis* reveals that the moon was always meant to serve as a *mekabel*, a receiver, and never a *nosein*, a giver. Rav Tzadok expands upon this basic concept.

Hashem created His world within the structure and format of *nosein* and *mekabel*. In a basic sense, Hashem serves as the ultimate *Nosein*, while Man serves as the ultimate *mekabel*. This relationship exists between the sun and the moon as well. The sun was to be the *nosein* and source of light, while the moon was to be the *mekabel* and reflect it to Earth. Rav Tzadok explains that the complaint that the moon had regarding the two kings with one crown refers to the bond that is being established when the moon accepts all the light of the sun and therefore is also considered complete and full. The relationship of the sun and moon as *nosein* and *mekabel* represents the ultimate relationship of Hashem as the *Nosein* and mankind—Klal Yisrael—as the *mekabel*. In the state where the moon is accepting all the light of the sun, the implication is that the *mekabel* is able to receive all that is being offered by the *nosein*—that the *mekablim*, mankind, is able to be *mekabel* all that the *Nosein*, Hashem, is offering. The moon said that this wasn't possible. There is going to be evil in the world, and then mankind will be spiritually incapable of being *mekabel* all of the *shefa*, Divine influence, that Hashem is willing to bestow upon Man. The appearance of the moon as always full would project such a state; this is what the moon rightfully declared couldn't exist, and this is what Hashem agreed with. By telling the *mekabel*, the moon, to diminish itself during the course of the month, Hashem was acknowledging that this was to be the unfortunate reality in an imperfect world. Thus, it wasn't that the moon was meant to be a source of light, but rather, it was originally designated to be physically able to be *mekabel* all of the *ohr* of the sun. It is this state which could and will exist in a world which totally recognizes the *Malchus*, the Kingship of Hashem.

The Yamim Tovim are all celebrated on the fifteenth of the month or based upon it. Pesach is on the fifteenth of the month of Nissan when the moon is full, and the Yom Tov of Sukkos is on the fifteenth day of Tishrei. Shavuos is specifically fifty days after the fifteenth of the month of Nissan (the reason it is fifty is a most profound idea but is not relevant for discussion at this point). The Yamim Tovim are called "good days" for they are meant to establish and lead the world to *yemos haMashiach*, the time when all mankind will recognize that Hashem is indeed *Echad*, the One and Only. At that time, the *mekablim* will be able to accept all the *ohr* of the *Nosein*, Hashem. Indeed, the excitement of each Rosh Chodesh, the first day of the month, when there is a new moon, is that perhaps this will be the month when the moon will reappear and grow to its *sheleimus* and remain full forever. This would signify the *sheleimus*, the complete state of spiritual perfection, that the *mekablim* have reached to be *mekabel* all that the *Nosein* has to offer. When that day does come, the moon will stay full, for the world will have reached its *tachlis*, its absolute state of fulfillment. It will have emerged from its state of darkness to the light of reflecting the *ohr* of the *Nosein*. Such is the way with regard to the moon, and such is true with regard to Man, Klal Yisroel. It is our spiritual mission, destiny, and hope, that we will **emerge** from our state of spiritual imperfection to one of *sheleimus* and the capacity to cleave to Hashem *l'netzach netzachim*, for all eternity.

Darkness

WHEN WE WAKE up in the morning, we naturally feel that this is the start of a new day. Yet, in regard to Jewish law, the day begins the night before. In this quality lies something that defines the very essence of our *avodas Hashem*.

The secular calendar regards the day as starting in the morning. Within the secular world, there are modes of behavior and rules that govern our actions. These sometimes have reasons, such as the beginning of the day starting when we awake from our sleep, and sometimes do not have significant reasons; rather, they are established arbitrarily. This is not the case with that which relates to Judaism. Whether we are privy to the reasons or not, Judaism is based on the Will of Hashem and therefore has intrinsic meaning. In order to understand this point, we must cite something mentioned in the first discussion in the Gemara in *Berachos*.

The Gemara asks: Why does the *Masechta* begin with the time of the mitzvah of saying the *Shema Yisrael* at night? It should first deal with when we are required to recite it by day. The Gemara answers that the Tanna of the Mishnah followed the order in which day is described at the creation of the world. The *pasuk* in *Parashas Bereishis* says: "It was evening and it was morning one day."[1] Thus, in a sense, the Torah is

---

1 *Bereishis* 1:5.

revealing to us that in the true reality, night precedes day. The *Maharal* in *Netzach Yisrael* explains the logic as to *why* this is true.

The *Maharal* begins his *sefer* by discussing a situation in which we must first deal with a state of imperfection and only then with the state of perfection, as this is the nature of how Hashem created His world. The mitzvah of *Maggid*—the discussion of the wonders and miracles that we are commanded to relate at the Seder of the first night(s) of Pesach—begins with *gnai*, shame and embarrassment, and ends with *shevach*, praise. We begin our recital with words that describe how our forefathers were slaves and idol worshippers—a state of imperfection—and end by describing the redemption and wonders of *yetzias Mitzrayim*—a state of perfection.

Sefarim also deal with the specific style of the dialogue. As every child knows, the high point of the night is when the youngest child recites the *Mah Nishtanah*—the four questions as to why this night is different from all of the other nights of the year. Following the questions, the answer begins. Here, too, we see the progression from imperfection (lack of understanding, questions) to that of perfection (answers). The questions represent a state of wonder and bewilderment, which are then satisfied by the proper responses.

On a basic level, the *Maharal* explains that "*Yedias hafuchim achas*"—the ability to understand anything requires a true and thorough clarity of its opposite. Thus, in order to truly appreciate the wonders of being free and existing as Hashem's nation, there must first be an acknowledgment of the slavery of our forefathers, as well as their involvement in other forms of worship. As every teacher and student can testify, to truly understand an answer, the question has to be dealt with in all its terms. Still, there is more. The *Maharal* adds an additional insight that is directly related to the question of night and day.

The words in *Bereishis*, "It was evening and it was morning one day," are not merely discussing the order of the parts of the day, but rather encapsulate the full dimension of Hashem's role and intent in creating the world. Hashem created beings that are, by definition as creations, inherently flawed and imperfect. This creature, Man, although imperfect, was given the wherewithal to develop from his state of imperfection to the highest state possible of human perfection. The vehicle to achieve this lofty goal of perfection is through one's study of Torah and his performance of mitzvos. Through our *avodah* we earn our reward and existence in *Olam Haba*. *Olam Haba* is a world of perfection, and therefore, our life in *Olam Hazeh* is to establish our ability to exist in the true realm of perfection. Thus, everything exists within this framework. Man develops through his *avodah*. Klal Yisrael also exists within such a process and therefore must first experience the *galus*, the state of imperfection, and only then the sense of spirituality provided through the input of Hashem, which will usher in the *geulah*, redemption. It is this idea that explains the true sequence of night and day.

In an imperfect world, first one relates to the time of night replete with its inability to facilitate true functioning. After the exposure to imperfection, the input of Hashem affords the *sheleimus* and perfection of day.

Just as the world and Man must strive to develop their *sheleimus*, this aspect is being mirrored within the basic framework of the day. Therefore, in a Jewish day, first comes night and then, and only then, the light of day. This process can similarly be perceived within another relationship that resembles night and day—that of Yaakov and Eisav.

The *pasuk* in *Parashas Toldos* states: "The first one came out with a ruddy complexion, covered completely with what was like a hairy robe, and they named him Eisav. After that his brother came out, his hand grasping the heel of Eisav, and he [Yitzchak] named him Yaakov."[2] Eisav was born first and as a result, seemingly deserved the *bechorah*, birthright, as the firstborn of Yitzchak. Yaakov gave Eisav the *nezid adashim*, red pottage, in order to purchase the *bechorah* from him. Theoretically, if Hashem desired that Yaakov be considered the *bechor*, it would have been simpler for him to be born first and receive the *bechorah* in a natural way. Yet, Eisav was born first and his hatred for Yaakov developed out of Yaakov's purchase of the birthright. Why did Hashem orchestrate their birth in this way?

---

2 Ibid., 25:25.

In *Kabbalas Shabbos*, in the *Lechah Dodi* we recite, "*Sof maaseh, b'machshavah techilah*—Last in creation but first in thought." Rav Shlomo Alkabetz is explaining the awesome *kedushah* of Shabbos. Although it was last in deed, in the sense that it was the last of the seven days of creation, it was first in thought. The *kedushah* of *Shabbos* was created first and, in that sense, brought forth the physical world. This means that the goal of all creation lies in the *menuchah*, the ultimate rest that represents a sense of spiritual completion, which is the essence of the holiness of Shabbos. The physical realm was created to provide a place where *avodas Hashem* could exist within the challenges of *bechirah*, free choice, that are constantly present in our world. Through that *avodah*, the person will ultimately receive his *menuchah*—his sense of being and existence in the spiritual realm of *Olam Haba*. Thus, Shabbos is "*me'ein Olam Haba*" because it is the expression of the *menuchah* of *Olam Haba* in our mundane and hectic world. It is because Shabbos represents the totally spiritual realm of *Olam Haba* that it was revealed into *Olam Hazeh* last.

Rashi cites a midrash that reveals to us that Yaakov felt that his right to the *bechorah* was justified. Yaakov and Eisav were twins, and Yaakov had been conceived first. It is similar to two stones that were placed within a narrow tube with only one opening. That which enters first emerges last, while that which was placed second leaves first. Yaakov represents the spiritual *tachlis*, and as such, he was conceived first, just like Shabbos. Eisav was revealed and actually born first, for his domain was that of the revealed world. Rav Tzadok adds another dimension to this point.

In the ideal state of being, both Yaakov and Eisav were to create Klal Yisrael. Yaakov was to be the "*Ish Tam*," the one to portray spiritual perfection and serve as the *tachlis* of the pair. But Eisav was to have a role in the sense of being the "*Shomeres Ha'pri*," the protector to ensure that all is well within the *tachlis*. Fruits have shells and peels so that through them, the quality and integrity of their inner fruit can be preserved. The peel of an orange gets abused and soiled, but the inner core remains perfect. Such was to be the relationship between Yaakov and Eisav. Just as when one is prepared to enjoy an orange, first the peel is visible, and only then one comes to relate to its inner realm, so too Eisav entered the external world first, and then Yaakov emerged. Rav Tzadok adds that normally night precedes day within the normal framework of a day in Hashem's world. As the *pasuk* depicts in *maaseh Bereishis*, "It was evening and it was morning one day." First there was the mundane and sense of *he'edar*, the lack of a fulfilled experience represented by night, and then there was the bestowing of Hashem's Presence to give purpose, meaning, and a sense of *ohr*.

We see a contrast to this with regard to *kodshim*—the time allotted to the eating of *korbanos*—where we find that the night follows the day. Rav Tzadok explains that since *kodshim* are holy, their spiritual status is that of the hidden realm of *kedushah* and is comparative to the inner fruit of the *pri*. Thus, when one is, in a sense, inside the fruit, his initial exposure is to the core and fruit, and then subsequently he reaches the external shell. The goal of Man's existence is to live his life "*toch ha'pri*"—within the realm that constitutes the core and essence of the world. For once again, what is hidden represents the elements of *kedushah* that are similar to the light of day, while the external portrays the physical and mundane, similar to the darkness of night.

The *pasuk* in *Parashas Bereishis* says: "Hashem said: Let there be *me'oros*, lights, in the canopy of heaven to divide between the day and the night, and they will serve for signs for seasons, for days and for years...Hashem made the two great lights, the large light to rule the day, and the small light to rule the night and the stars."[3] *Rashi* explains in the name of Chazal that the sun and the moon were created equal, but after the moon complained, it was diminished in the sense that after the fifteenth of the month, it gets smaller and smaller until it is no longer visible. Then, at the beginning of the next month, it reappears again to grow, and the cycle repeats itself. *Rashi* explains that because Hashem diminished the size of the moon, He added the stars as part of its entourage to placate it. This raises a question. Considering that

---

3 Ibid., 1:15.

the additional light provided by the stars is actually very minimal, how does their presence serve to pacify the moon? There is clearly more to understand.

The explanation is based on the words of the *Gra*. Each morning, we recite in the first *berachah* of *birchas Krias Shema*: "*Yotzer ohr u'vorei choshech, oseh shalom u'vorei es ha'kol*—[Hashem] Who forms light, and creates darkness, makes peace and creates all," based on the words of Yeshayah.[4] In our terms, the first step in the development of an object is its creation—*briah*, and then it is formed—*yetzirah*, in the specific form you want for it. Thus, the realm that relates to something's creation is higher than that which relates to the realm where it is formed. It would therefore seem curious that Hashem *forms* light but *creates* darkness. The *pasuk* seems to indicate that the realm of darkness is above the realm of light, for it truly is.

To be clear, it is not the darkness itself that we sense is greater than the light, but rather that the "sense" of *ohr*, light, that exists at night is far greater than the light of the day. The light of the night is not physical: it is the light from the absolute realm of *kedushah* of beyond.

In the *Mah Nishtanah* that we recite at the Seder, we ask why this night is different from all other nights of the year. The *pasuk* in *Tehillim* states: "The darkness will not withhold anything from you, and the night will shine as the day."[5] The word *choshech*, darkness, comes from the word *chasach*, which means to hold back. The *pasuk* in *Parashas Vayeira*, directly after Avraham is told not to slaughter his son Yitzchak, says: "Do not touch the lad, nor do anything to harm him; for now I know that you are one who fears Hashem, *v'lo chasachta*—and you have not withheld your son, your only one from Me."[6] Darkness is not to be understood as the absence of *ohr*, but rather our inability to perceive the *ohr* that is being bestowed at night. The night of Pesach was indeed different because, that night, the *ohr* shined like day. It doesn't mean that the light of the sun was visible; rather, at that point, Klal Yisrael

---

4 *Yeshayah* 45:7.

5 *Tehillim* 139:12.

6 *Bereishis* 22:12.

was on the spiritual *madreigah*, level, to be able to relate to the *ohr* that emanates from the moon at night—the sense of *ohr* of the world of *tikkun*, perfection, of *Acharis HaYamim*, the End of Days, when the world will realize its spiritual potential, that Hashem is the Source of all existence. Rav Tzadok explains a profound idea relating to this point.

Chazal coined the phrase "*sagi nahar*" to describe a blind person, the strict definition of which is that the person has too much light. Why did they use this phrase? One could simply suggest that instead of saying that a blind person has no light, with its obvious tragic connotation, they chose to refer to it in the opposite sense. This is "*lashon sagi nahar*," a term that denotes the opposite of the literal meaning.

Rav Tzadok writes that this is a superficial understanding. He explains that a person may be blind for one of two reasons: either because he has no light or because he is blinded by too much light. Since the results are the same, Chazal chose to refer to one who is blind from too much light rather than the other alternative. The point for us is meaningful because, in a sense, the *ohr* at night bears a spiritual identity, and as such, we are unable to perceive it with our physical senses to actually recognize its existence. It is therefore considered *choshech*, held back from us, and we are unable to relate to it. The light of night is therefore more sublime and spiritual; it is a product of the realm of "*borei*"—the creation referred to in the *pasuk*. The light of day, while it enables us to actually see, is merely a function of the realm referred to as "*yotzer*" of that same *pasuk*. It is here that the stars play their all-important role.

In the *sefer Mamaarei Pachad Yitzchak* on Sukkos, Rav Yitzchok Hutner explains the key to understanding the "*piyus ha'levanah*—the appeasement of the moon." The moon reigns at the time when this holy and profound *ohr* is being bestowed upon the world. But as we know, it doesn't provide the kind of physical light one would utilize for one's daily functioning. One might mistakenly assume that there is no light at night and that the sun is paramount, the sole source of light dwelling in the heavens, for how can the light of the moon ever compare to it? In truth, though, the moon *is* comparable—and even goes beyond. The night can be compared to a tent that blocks out all light. One sitting in the tent would assume it is absolutely dark, but if he were to prick little holes in its roof, specks of light would be able to shine through to reveal that, indeed, there is light beyond. Similarly, the stars twinkle in the night to hint to us that there is a light beyond. All is not bleak. The *piyus ha'levanah* lies in the stars' revelation that there truly is *ohr* present that is being bestowed, but because of its totally spiritual and holy source, we aren't able to relate to it. The presence of the stars proclaims to us that this spiritual light does exist and that it is only present during the *malchus* of the *levanah*. As such, the *levanah* is appeased.

One cannot speak of darkness without mentioning *Makkas Choshech*, the plague of darkness that struck the Egyptians as one of the ten *Makkos*. We understand that the plague of darkness wasn't simply an inability to see. Perhaps in a basic sense, we could compare it to being punished in solitary confinement, or worse. During *Makkas Choshech*, people who stood couldn't sit, and those sitting were locked in that position and afraid to move. There was an intense feeling of isolation and of being excluded from existence. The *Avnei Nezer* identifies the essence of this darkness and the qualities of torment it created.

The *pasuk* in *Tehillim* says: "He sent darkness and made it dark, and they did not challenge his word."[7] Chazal reveal to us that the reason the Egyptians were punished was because they failed to heed the word of Hashem. In order to explain these words, the *Avnei Nezer* cites the words of the *Kedushas Levi*, the Berditchiver.

The Berditchiver explains that this *choshech*, darkness, was not merely the absence of light. *Midrash Rabbah* in *Parashas Bo* asks from where this darkness came and answers, from the "*choshech shel Maalah*—the darkness of Above." The *pasuk* in *Tehillim* says: "He [Hashem] made darkness His camouflage."[8] In our terms, the *choshech* of *Maalah* represents the *ohr ha'ganuz*, hidden spiritual light, that is beyond Man's ability to relate to. In a sense, it is not merely something we are not able to absorb; rather, it is a dimension of *ohr* that would negate any creature not spiritually

7 *Tehillim* 105:28.
8 Ibid., 18:12.

fitting that came into contact with it. As we saw above, the words in Aramaic that Chazal coined to refer to a blind person are *sagi nahar*. The word *sagi* means "much," and we explained that one of the ways in which one's sight is restricted is if one is blinded by an overwhelming amount of light. The *choshech shel Maalah* represents this *ohr*, which by nature must be *chashuch*—restricted and withheld from the eyes of mankind.

At the *Akeidah*, the *pasuk* in which Avraham Avinu did not hold back his beloved son Yitzchak from becoming a *korban* says: "For now I know that you are one who fears Hashem, *v'lo* ***chasachta***—since you have not **withheld** your son, your only one from Me." Thus, the word *choshech* is to be understood as the overwhelming holy *ohr* from Above that must be withheld from mankind lest it destroy them. It is thereby perceived as the state of darkness. Vessels can only contain a certain quantity; when there is an overabundance, they are subject to breaking. It was this *choshech shel Maalah* that served as the plague of darkness.

The *pasuk* referring to *Makkas Choshech* says: "No man could see his brother, nor could anyone rise from his place for a three-day period; but for all B'nei Yisrael, there was light in their dwellings."[9] The *pasuk* doesn't say that in the houses of B'nei Yisrael there was no darkness, but rather that there was *ohr.* At that point they were *zocheh* to an *ohr* that was far beyond their *madreigah* because they were spiritually preparing themselves to be redeemed. They were to become the nation to exist *l'netzach*, for eternity, with Hashem and were thus deemed fit to relate to such an *ohr*. The Gemara in *Avodah Zarah* states that in *Acharis HaYamim*, Hashem will remove the sun from its shell; through this *ohr*, the *reshaim*, evildoers, will be punished, while the *tzaddikim* will be healed. The same *ohr* will be destructive to some, but to those who are spiritually fit, only good will result. Therefore, there was *ohr* in the homes of B'nei Yisrael, but torment in the houses of the Egyptians.

Chazal on the *pasuk* in *Tehillim* reveal to us that Hashem sent the Egyptians *Makkas Choshech* because they didn't listen to His words. Had they accepted the responsibility to listen to the word of Hashem, they

---

9 *Shemos* 10:23.

would have prepared themselves spiritually to accept the sovereignty of Hashem as well. Because they didn't, they could not relate to the *ohr shel Maalah* in any fashion whatsoever, and therefore, as a result of too much *ohr*, they as vessels "broke" and suffered from the plague of darkness.

B'nei Yisrael, however, were able to receive this *ohr*, and in their homes there was indeed light.

In light of the above, it is fascinating that the four-fifths of B'nei Yisrael that were killed in Mitzrayim died specifically during *Makkas Choshech*. It wasn't perchance, but rather as a result of what was being bestowed upon B'nei Yisrael at that point.

At the beginning of *Parashas Beshalach*, the *pasuk* says: "And so *Elokim* led the people round, by way of the Red Sea Desert, and B'nei Yisrael went up *chamushim*, armed, from the land of Egypt." *Rashi* explains that the word *chamushim* (related to the word *chamesh*, meaning "five") reveals to us that only one of every five went out of Mitzrayim, and that four-fifths died during the three days of darkness. *Rashi* in *Parashas Bo* reveals to us that they died during the days of darkness in order that the Mitzriyim shouldn't see that many of B'nei Yisrael were killed as well. Perhaps we can understand an additional idea that is being represented by the exact timing and method of their deaths. To appreciate this point, we must first discuss what occurred in the plague of darkness.

The *Malbim* in *Shemos* reveals to us that the *choshech* that Hashem brought was a function of the *ohr ha'ganuz*, the original light that was revealed at the creation of the world that Hashem subsequently hid, as we mentioned above. *Rashi* in *Parashas Bereishis* explains that Hashem saw that it was not fitting that the wicked should have use of this great light and therefore hid it and designated it for the righteous in *Olam Haba*. *Sefarim* explain that just as the regular light that brightens our world gives one the ability to physically relate to things, so too, the original great *ohr* gave one the ability to perceive the absolute truth of Hashem's creation. Through it, one could relate to everything that exists. The question is asked, if it was truly dark during the days of the plague of darkness, how did B'nei Yisrael have the ability to see at all? This, the *Malbim* explains, was possible through Hashem revealing the *ohr ha'ganuz*.

The light of day gives us the capacity to see the world through physical human senses. All healthy humans can see by day, and in a sense, all spiritually "healthy" people could potentially be privy to the *ohr ha'ganuz*. What occurred during the plague of darkness was that the spiritual light of the *ohr ha'ganuz* was so great, the evil Mitzriyim weren't able to "see" with it.

Rav Tzadok explains that the choice of the term *sagi nahar* to refer to one who is blind is exact. One can be blinded in a situation of no *ohr*, as well as too much *ohr*. Such was the case in the days of the plague of darkness—there was an overabundance of light, and the Mitzriyim could not relate to it; therefore, all was dark. Perhaps what plagued the Mitzriyim had tragic consequences for a major portion of B'nei Yisrael, and as a result, four-fifths died during those days as well.

The *pasuk* that depicts the death of the firstborns of Mitzrayim states: "This is what Hashem has said, 'About the time of midnight, I will go out in the midst of Egypt. *U'meis kol bechor*—And every firstborn in the land of Egypt will die.'"[10] Rav Tzadok, in his *sefer Resisei Laylah*, points out that the Torah doesn't say that Hashem will kill them; rather, when Hashem's Presence is revealed in Mitzrayim, the Mitzriyim will die as a result. The tremendous level of *kedushah* being revealed will be too much for them to relate to, and they will therefore simply cease to exist. This is similar to what occurs through the water drunk by the *sotah*, the woman suspected of acting immorally. The *Avnei Nezer* explains that what she drinks doesn't kill her directly; rather, it contains an overwhelming dimension of *kedushah*:

- If she is worthy and has not sinned, the water will bring her great blessings.
- If she has sinned, her body will not be able to absorb and relate to the *kedushah*, and she will therefore die. The Gemara even

---

10 Ibid., 11:4–5.

> explains that the parts of her body that were involved in her sin will be subject to destruction first because the *tumah*, spiritual uncleanliness, created by her immoral actions permeates her body in different proportions, thus disabling her capacity to relate to the profound *kedushah* inherent in the water.

The *Avnei Nezer* focuses on the Kohen's role in administering the punishment of the *sotah*, yet the Torah refers to the Kohen as "*ish chasidecha*—your man of kindness."[11] Thus, if she has indeed acted immorally, we are not to consider what befalls her a direct form of punishment that comes through the Kohen; rather, he is enabling her to receive a great spiritual infusion—to the point that if she hasn't sinned, she will be the recipient of profound blessings. But if she is guilty, her physical body will not be able absorb the exalted *kedushah* she experiences, and she will therefore succumb. Perhaps this may also be true for those who weren't part of the *chamushim* that left Mitzrayim.

At the time that they were to be redeemed from their *shibud*, slavery, in Mitzrayim, B'nei Yisrael lacked the performance of mitzvos necessary to provide them with the proper spiritual merit to be freed. What was required of them was their desire to be part of the nation of Klal Yisrael. Hashem had sworn to the Avos—Avraham, Yitzchak, and Yaakov—that He would take their descendents out of their bondage in Mitzrayim. But those children of the Avos who didn't want to be redeemed were not able to relate to the spiritual greatness that was being revealed at that point. Their desire to connect with the Avos and be part of the nation being created at yetzias Mitzrayim was to be the foundation of Bnei Yisrael, enabling their capacity to relate to the kedushah and *ohr* being revealed during the three days of *choshech*. By their unwillingness to become part of such a nation, they were subject to the blinding that defines the lashon of *saghi nahar*. The Mitzriyim weren't destined for greatness and thus didn't perish during the plague of *choshech*. But the members of B'nei Yisrael were destined to spiritually soar; in that which they were opposed to be part of the nation, the result of the *ohr*

---

11 *Devarim* 33:8.

being revealed at that point resulted in their death. Thus, they ceased to exist specifically during the days of *Makkas Choshech* as a result of their inability to properly relate to the level of *kedushah* being revealed to the budding nation of Klal Yisrael.

Midrash Rabbah at the beginning of *Parashas Mikeitz* states on the *pasuk* in *Iyov*: "*Keitz sam l'choshech…*—He [Hashem] sets an end to the darkness, and He investigates the end of everything."[12] What is the "end" that Hashem establishes?

Yosef was in jail, locked up amid the *tumah* of Mitzrayim, and Hashem redeemed him from his plight. He became the viceroy of the land and was in charge of feeding all of its inhabitants during the years of famine. The time had come for Yosef to be saved, when he was to see the light emerging from the end of his darkness. The *Beis HaLevi* in his *kuntres* on *Mitzvas Bitachon*, basing himself upon this *pasuk* in *Iyov*, reveals the true message of living in darkness and subsequently being freed.

What is darkness? The simple answer is that darkness is a state that represents the absence of light. But the *pasuk* in *Yeshayah* seems to imply differently: "[I am Hashem,] *yotzer ohr u'vorei choshech*—Who forms light and creates darkness." The *Navi* is telling us that Hashem actively creates *choshech*; it does not merely exist when *ohr* is removed.

In *Nefesh HaChaim*, Rav Chaim Volozhiner explains that the creation of *choshech* is even more profound than that of its counterpart, *ohr*. There are four basic worlds that exist: *atzilus*, *briah*, *yetzirah*, and the world we inhabit, *asiah*. The most exalted and spiritual is that of *atzilus*, while the lowest is our world of *asiah*. *Briah* is the second-most holy world and is more spiritual than *yetzirah*. The *pasuk* above is referring to the **formation** of *ohr* with *yotzer*, as emanating from the world of *yetzirah*, while *choshech* is **created** from the world of *briah*, implied by the word *borei*. What is this darkness whose status emerges from the (second) world of *briah*? The *Sfas Emes* teaches us a profound *yesod,* principle, regarding the concept of *choshech*.

---

12 *Iyov* 28:3.

During *yom*, day, the *ohr* that Hashem bestows upon the world can be processed by the world. *Ohr* represents a form and dimension of light, and during the day, its level is such that we humans in our physical world retain the capacity to experience it and relate to it.

But during *laylah*, night, the level of *ohr* being released is from *briah*, a higher level, and is beyond our spiritual capacity to perceive. Thus, at night when we cannot see without physical light, all seems to be cloaked in darkness. *Choshech* represents a *kisui*, covering, which conceals and hides the enormous *ohr* that exists during *laylah*. The midrash is teaching us that as long as the many aspects that portray a sense of *choshech* exist in the world, the *ohr* of Hashem cannot be discerned. The *yetzer hara*, Man's evil inclination, clouds his ability to sense truth in the world that Hashem created. When the time arrives for Hashem to destroy the *yetzer hara*, the darkness will cease, and Man will recognize his Creator. Thus, darkness represents Man's inability to recognize the Presence of Hashem. It is this idea that the *pasuk* in *Iyov* is revealing to us.

As long as Yosef was in jail, he dwelled within darkness, unable to perceive *Hashem* to the fullest capacity. When the time came for the darkness to cease, Hashem orchestrated the process through which Yosef was ultimately to be freed through Pharaoh's dream. The *Beis HaLevi* explains that this is the proper way for us to understand the meaning of our own personal sense of darkness and its end.

"*Keitz sam l'choshech*"—there was a specific time for Yosef to be in jail. Whatever the *cheshbon* was, the time that he had to endure his own private bondage and darkness was totally according to the *ratzon Hashem*. Since this represented the decree of Hashem, there was nothing that he or anyone else could have done to nullify it. The moment Hashem wanted Yosef to be released from jail, the scene was set for Pharaoh's dream, resulting in Yosef's freedom. However, the *Beis HaLevi* writes that we shouldn't think that Yosef was set free as a result of Pharaoh's dream, which served as the cause. Rather, Hashem decreed that Yosef should be free, and so Pharaoh had the dream to enable *ratzon Hashem* to come to fruition. It was the goal of setting Yosef free that caused Pharaoh to have the dream, and not the other way round. With this *yesod*, he answers another complex issue with regard to Yosef and his brothers.

The *pasuk* in *Parashas Vayeishev* states: "Yisrael loved Yosef more than any of his sons, for he was a son of his old age, and he made him a *kesones pasim*, a colorful cloak."[13] The *Beis HaLevi* tells us openly that we should not make the mistake of thinking that the *kesones pasim* was the cause of Yosef being sold to Mitzrayim and the subsequent *galus* of B'nei Yisrael. Rather, Hashem had revealed His decree to Avraham Avinu during the *Bris Bein Habesarim*, informing him that his children would be in exile for many years in a land that was not theirs. This decree had to be fulfilled, and the vehicle was the *kesones pasim*, along with the negative feelings it created among the holy children of Yaakov Avinu. If there would never have been a *kesones pasim*, the decree would have been accomplished through another vehicle.

This is a profound principle. There are many instances in the course of our lives where we would do well to remember the words of the *Beis HaLevi*. We are constantly faced with situations that we mistakenly label as "causes" for some unfortunate "result" that has befallen us.

But this is not how the world really works; it is not true in the ultimate sense of Truth. Hashem's decree is the cause of our situation, and He is the address to which we should direct our concern. The Gemara in *Masechta Niddah*[14] quotes the words of Rav Simlai. "*Darash Rav Simlai*"—Rav Simlai taught that the time when a fetus is growing within its mother is the ideal time of life. The child's nourishment is secure because it comes directly from his mother, and no one is able to take it away from him. Similarly, there is no way for him to get that which is external to his own private world and for him to be able to take away that which is destined for another. The *Maharal* reveals an added dimension to these profound words. It's not that while the child is a fetus all is good, and that when it enters the "real world" everything sours, and the child is now subject to the rough and tough of our realm.

13 *Bereishis* 37:3.
14 30b.

Rather, what occurs with the developing fetus represents the true nature of that person's sense of existence on earth.

The fetus lives in a clear-cut reality with all his needs being taken care of. No one can take his sustenance from him, and he cannot take from anyone else. Hashem established this system in order for a person to recognize that this is the situation of all of us during the time when we are alive in *Olam Hazeh*. An *adam gadol* once explained that we all think that everyone else is privy to the "bubble" that represents the nature of our own life. Hashem created our bubble, and we think that our lives function as a Venn diagram with overlapping parts. What I have is not secure, and perhaps I can get what the other person is also striving for. Rav Simlai is revealing to us that this is not truth. What Hashem has decreed for each of us is ours, and no one can take it away. Hashem established each of us with our own private bubble that no one else can infiltrate, and in the same vein, no one can take what exists in the bubble of another. What happens to a fetus reflects our entire existence. It isn't that when we are born, we have the misfortune to be brought to this tough world; rather, we are to glean from our early existence the truth of what we can expect and what we cannot. The famous words of the *Ibn Ezra* reflect this idea when he discusses the commandment of "*Lo sachmod*—Do not covet."

There are certain things that we must appreciate are beyond our grasp—Hashem has decreed that they are not to be considered as part of our bubble, and we therefore have absolutely no connection to those things. The simple person from a village has no true chance of marrying the princess, and he should therefore not covet her. If we realize something is truly beyond us, it is not part of our realm and should not produce the feelings of wishing to attain them. If Hashem's ultimate decree is no, then *nothing* in the world can create the capacity for us to acquire it. It is only Hashem who can put an end to the darkness.

We are accustomed to thinking of darkness and light in terms of the physical world we live in. But when the Torah discusses *choshech* and *ohr*, we must realize that it is referring to a spiritual dimension as well.

In the beginning of *Parashas Vayeishev*, *Rashi* cites the midrash that says that Yaakov was seeking to live *b'shalvah*, in tranquility, when the troubles of Yosef were thrust upon him. *Rashi* adds that Hashem said: "Is it not enough for the righteous to have what was designated for them in *Olam Haba*, that they should also want to live in tranquility in this world?"[15] These words of Chazal establish a certain premise in terms of the proper way to relate to *Olam Haba*—as well as to *Olam Hazeh*.

The *pasuk* in *Parashas Bereishis* that introduces the day of Shabbos states: "*Elokim* completed on the seventh day His work which He had made."[16] *Rashi* focuses on the idea that Hashem actually finished what He had intended to create on Shabbos itself. He explains that there was indeed one element that the world was still lacking after the six days of creation—*menuchah*, rest—and with the arrival of Shabbos, the concept of rest was created.

What does it mean that there was no concept of rest until Shabbos? One would assume that the capacity to build a couch upon which to recline was established within the first six days of physical creation. But the point of the novelty called *menuchah* is that the development of something could *stop*, signifying that it has reached its potential.

Within our mundane world, all physical things are created as pure potential. They are meant to be developed to reveal and realize their spiritual potential and thereby accomplish the purpose that Hashem intended when He created them. The world is constantly developing from *ko'ach el ha'poel*, from potential to the state of the realization of the goal intended. Such is the meaning of *Olam Hazeh*, the realm where all things are meant to develop in their specific form of *kavod Shamayim* from potential to reality. Here lies the *chiddush* of Shabbos.

Although the seventh day of the week is seemingly part of the fiber of the physical world, it serves to represent the world of *sechar* of *Olam Haba*. It is considered "*Me'ein Olam Haba*"—a glimmer of the world of reward that Hashem, in His kindness, granted us as part of the *Olam Hazeh* in which we presently exist. The essence of the reward we will be

---

15 *Bereishis* 37:2.

16 Ibid, 2:3.

zocheh to in *Olam Haba* is the *b'po'el*, the realization of the spiritual potential we had in *Olam Hazeh*. Thus, the concept of true rest cannot exist in *Olam Hazeh*. All through our lives, we are granted the opportunity to constantly develop that potential to create the sense of *menuchah*, of having fulfilled our spiritual destiny that serves as our existence in *Olam Haba*.

The above concept is connected to the idea that the soul of Man is compared to a candle. The *pasuk* in *Mishlei* states: "Man's soul is the lamp of Hashem."[17] *Sefarim* explain that the nature of a flame is that it is never at rest. It is constantly flickering upward. This portrays two profound insights with regard to our souls and the meaning of our lives.

First, fire represents a situation of potential being realized. The light is considered locked up within the oil; it must be developed in order for it to be utilized and thereby reach its potential. Interestingly, the *pasuk* in *Parashas Vayakhel* that discusses the prohibition of doing halachic work on Shabbos refers to the kindling of fire. The *pasuk* says: "You must not kindle a fire in all your dwelling places on the day of Shabbos."[18] The kindling of fire represents the exact opposite of the sense of *kedushas Shabbos*:

- Shabbos represents the realization of all spiritual potential.
- Fire is the process of the actual development. It personifies the *melachah* that is contrary to and defies *kedushas Shabbos*.

Similarly, our souls are created with enormous potential, the realization of which serves as our life's quest. There is an additional aspect in that a flame is in constant motion flickering upward.

Hashem could have created a flame to move in any direction, but the fact that it soars upward represents its own personal yearning to reconnect with its own *shoresh*, source of existence. The *Sefas Emes* explains that Hashem created a world composed of the four *yesodos*, basic elements: *afar*, earth; *mayim*, water; *avir*, air (or wind); and *aish*, fire. The *shoresh* of *aish* is in heaven, and therefore, the flame that is lit

17 *Mishlei* 20:27.

18 *Shemos* 35:3.

on earth seeks to reconnect with its source in heaven. The soul of Man is compared to a flame because it too *must* exist in perpetual motion if it seeks to develop its spiritual destiny. And just as fire aspires to reconnect with its own *shoresh*, so is the pursuit of Man's existence in the temporary world of *Olam Hazeh*. While we are here, we must strive, which is why in the physical world, peace and tranquility are not the flavor of the day. *Olam Haba* is the ultimate *menuchah*, and it is then where peace and tranquility will reign for all eternity through our *deveikus* and connection with our Source—Hashem. While we all seek peace, it is not to be achieved in this world; rather, it is to serve as the essence of the *sechar*, reward, for a life of sincere *avodas Hashem*.

The *Ramchal* in *Mesillas Yesharim* writes that we need the things that make up our world to enable us to serve Hashem. The serenity that we seek plays a positive role when it provides us with the peace of mind that allows us to do what we were created to do.

But ultimately, the state of *shalvah* is not meant for now, but rather for our eternal existence in *Olam Haba*. There we will be ready to relate to the true light for all eternity through our *neshamah* connecting back with its *Shoresh*—Hashem—and the spiritual *ohr* that will radiate all existence, providing a guiding light to a world initially full of darkness.

We have seen that the World to Come is a world of true and eternal light. Our world has some elements of light, but it is essentially a world of darkness. It is this reality that plays a vital role in terms of the development of Mashiach in *Olam Hazeh*.

Interestingly, the relationships leading to the birth of Mashiach—such as Yehudah and Tamar, and David and Bas Sheva—seemingly occurred within problematic situations. The development of the lineage of Mashiach represents light, and as such, one would assume it would be built upon foundations that openly display a sense of spiritual perfection. But since that is not the case, we need to discover what the birth of Mashiach is meant to accomplish in terms of perfecting our world.

The *Maharal* teaches that "*Devarim gedolim einam b'mikrah*—Great events are not mere coincidence."[19] If something occurs through a certain process, we are to understand that it specifically had to be this way. Although the relationships leading to the birth of Mashiach appear problematic, in terms of actual halachah, they are not. To properly understand this idea, we will discuss the steps leading to the development of Mashiach.

The step that began this process was when Lot engaged in relations with his two daughters. From his actions, the two nations of Amon and Moav were born. These are the nations from which Rus (Moav) and Naama (Amon)—the mother of Rechavam, the son of Shlomo HaMelech—developed the chain of *malchus beis David*. The *Rambam* writes that in terms of *arayos*, improper relationships, a daughter is not considered an *ervah*, morally forbidden to her non-Jewish father.[20] Although Lot was spurned for what he did, technically, it wasn't considered a prohibited act for a gentile .

Chazal reveal to us that the daughters acted *l'sheim Shamayim*, for the sake of Heaven. They assumed that mankind was being destroyed as in the days of Noach, and they were the only humans left to survive and continue the world. *Sefarim* explain that as a result of their good intentions, the daughters of Amon and Moav who convert are permitted to immediately marry members of Klal Yisrael, while male converts of these two nations may not. Lot, however, was aware of the true nature of the limited destruction of the evil city of Sodom; thus, his intentions are not considered *l'sheim Shamayim*. Therefore, step one, although problematic, was not technically an act of *cheit*, sin.

The incident involving Yehudah and his daughter-in-law Tamar also survives scrutiny. Before *Matan Torah*, the giving of the Torah on Har Sinai, the act of *yibum*—when a man dies childless and his wife is commanded to marry a member of his family—could be accomplished even by the father of the deceased husband, and not only with his brother. Thus, technically speaking, Yehudah was performing the

---

19 *Maharal Tiferes Yisrael*, 25.

20 *Hilchos Isurei Biah*, chap. 14.

mitzvah of *yibum* in his actions with Tamar. Chazal reveal to us that Yehudah did not intend to go anywhere near Tamar, but the angel that is "*Me'muneh*"—appointed and in charge of desires—led him to her. Here again, although the external situation looked very problematic, Hashem was actually controlling the destinies of the people involved to create the capacity for the soul of Mashiach to enter the world.

Dovid HaMelech's relationship with Bas Sheva, seemingly a married woman, also seems to be problematic. But actually, it wasn't. The Gemara in *Masechta Kesubos* teaches us that the soldiers who fought for David HaMelech would write *gittin*, writs of divorce, to ensure that if they failed to return from the war and no one knew what had happened to them, their wives would be permitted to remarry. Here again, although the incident seems awkward, it was not inherently prohibited according to halachah. While certain aspects of the incident required David to do *teshuvah*, he was not technically guilty of immorality. *Sefarim* explain that David's sin was to have Uriah, Bas Sheva's first husband, killed in the specific manner that he was, as the *pasuk* states: "And him [Uriah] you killed with the sword of the children of Amon."[21] Uriah was "*mored b'malchus*"—he rebelled against King David and deserved to die. He should have been put to death within the proper framework of one who violated halachah, but David had him killed on the battlefront. This is the empowerment of the *avodah zarah* of B'nei Amon, and this is the primary sin for which David is held culpable in connection with Uriah's death. Thus, although externally the incident of David and Bas Sheva was of concern, the internal mechanism was legitimate.

Indeed, in each of these incidents, which form the background to the birth of Mashiach, the external events appeared challenging, but the internal Halachic reality was nevertheless correct. The key to understanding this process lies in the words of Rav Chaim Vital in his *sefer Eitz Hadas Tov*.

This development is directly opposite to that which occurred when the snake instigated the sin of Adam HaRishon. The *pasuk* in *Parashas*

---

21 *Shmuel II* 12:9.

Bereishis states: "The serpent was slyer (*arum*) than any beast of the field that Hashem made."[22] *Rashi* explains that the *nachash*, serpent, used his guile to trick Chavah into eating from the *Eitz Ha'daas*, the Tree of Knowledge. The *nachash* asked Chavah if Hashem had told them not to eat from all the trees of the garden. Although he saw Adam and Chavah eating from all the other trees and knew it was permissible, the *nachash* indulged her in conversation in order to get her to speak about the *Eitz Ha'daas*. The *nachash* had to utilize the craft of *urmah*, guile, to accomplish his goal of causing Adam and Chavah to sin.

Hashem had just created the world, and there was one commandment placed upon Adam: not to eat from the tree that was in the center of the garden. He was created *yashar*, spiritually straight on a path to naturally serve his Creator and not bend to the distortion of *cheit*. The evil inclination was external to Man, rather than within him; it was the *nachash* who was to tempt the newly created humans. Adam had the ability to follow evil, and that was his *bechirah*—his freedom of choice and the framework of his *avodah*. Into such a spiritual realm walked the *nachash*. His job was to challenge Adam, and challenge him he did. But the flavor of the challenge could not be easily perceived, otherwise there was no chance of Adam and Chavah succumbing. Therefore, he came with *urmah*. He openly talked about the commandments of Hashem, but secretly he steered the conversation to the tree. Externally what he did was correct, but internally it was evil. In a world of holiness, only through *urmah* is it possible to enable evil to dominate. Had he openly attempted to spiritually destroy Chavah, she would have recognized his true evil nature and thwarted him. Therefore, he came with cunning and through it allowed the fruits of evil to flourish. The development of Mashiach, leading us to a world of light, must be realized in a similar fashion—but in the opposite way.

In the world after the *cheit* of Adam HaRishon, it isn't the Adam of "*yashar*" that is dominant; it is the forces of evil and darkness that defy the truth of Hashem. To openly create a system that in a sense defies the

---

22 *Bereishis* 3:1.

very foundations of a world permeated by evil is impossible. The forces of darkness do not allow the seeds of light to bear fruit. Whether in a physical sense or within the realm of the spiritual through the actions of the Satan, who is appointed to represent the forces of *rah*, evil, in this world, *tov*, goodness, needs privacy to be nurtured and developed. When situations that seem somewhat problematic all lead to the growth of the ultimate state of *tov*—a world where all will recognize the Kingship of Hashem—we too are witnessing *urmah*. But this is *urmah* at its best. This explains why these externally problematic unions were actually essential for the development of Mashiach—because in our world of darkness, light must somehow develop amid the presence of evil.

There is another example of where *urmah* was necessary to ensure the process of ultimate *tikkun* would unfold as it should. When Yaakov received the *berachos* from his father, Yitzchak thought initially that he was blessing Eisav. Yaakov's receiving of the blessings was a major step in the creation of the ideal world. Yaakov came before his father Yitzchak with guile, for here too, the world of evil could not be openly defied. Just as the soul is hidden deep within the body, so too, all that leads to the ultimate *tov* must be subject to a process that shuns the external limelight. This is the secret of the birth of Melech HaMashiach, for only within the midst of darkness can light develop and ultimately be brought to fruition.

Difficulties

THE PASUK IN *Parashas Mikeitz* states: "Take your brother, get up, and return to the man. May the Almighty, *Shakai*, grant you mercy before the man, that he may release to you your other brother together with Binyamin."[1] Shimon is being held captive, and Yaakov Avinu is told that the viceroy of Mitzrayim has decreed that the only way his children can purchase food there is if they bring their youngest brother, Binyamin, down to Mitzrayim with them. Yaakov is contemplating the potentially tragical consequences of this, and *Rashi* explains the choice of Hashem's name of *Shakai* in his *tefillah*: Yaakov was praying that He Who said to His universe, "Enough," may He say to his troubles, "Enough." Yaakov stated that he'd had no rest from trouble and suffering since the time of his youth. He had suffered with the troubles of Eisav, Lavan, the early death of Rachel, Shechem's attack on Dinah, the alleged death of Yosef, the retaining of Shimon, and now of Binyamin.

In what way can we understand the words of Yaakov Avinu? Yaakov, the culmination of the Avos—Avraham, Yitzchak, and Yaakov—wouldn't simply complain. The *Maharal* in *Derech Chaim* teaches us a profound idea regarding the Avos and the destiny of Klal Yisrael.

The story of each of the Avos is, in a sense, the ultimate history of their children, Klal Yisrael. Avraham Avinu's youth was fraught with suffering, as exemplified by Nimrod's attempt to kill him. The tide turned

1 *Bereishis* 43:13–14.

when Hashem revealed Himself to Avraham, and from then on, his life proved tranquil. Such was the early story of B'nei Yisrael. Through Mitzrayim and during their early years, they experienced pain, but from the time they were created as a nation, they were, in the *Maharal*'s words, "Subject to the blessings of Hashem." This calm period mirrored the rest of Avraham's life as well as the beginning of Yitzchak's. Toward the end of Yitzchak's life, tragedies began to reappear. The *pasuk* in *Parashas Toldos* says: "Yitzchak had grown old, and his eyesight dimmed and he could not see,"[2] for his life represented the stage at which peace ended for Klal Yisrael and they entered into *galus*. When Yaakov goes down to Mitzrayim and meets Pharaoh, Yaakov says to him: "Few and bad have been the days of my life."[3] Most of Yaakov's years until that point had been days of pain, for he represented the years of *galus* of Klal Yisrael. From the days of the *churban Beis Hamikdash* through the days of *galus Edom* that we are currently in, the tale of Klal Yisrael has often been one of woe. Yaakov Avinu had *tzaros*, troubles, and since we have the principle of "*maaseh avos siman l'banim*"—what the Avos experienced is what will eventually transpire to their children—we, B'nei Yisrael, are thereby subject to a similar fortune. It was in this context that Yaakov said his words to Yehudah, the guarantor of Binyamin.

The different names of Hashem portray the different qualities of how Hashem reveals Himself to the world. The *sefarim* write that the *gematria*, numerical value, of the word *Shemo*, His name, is 346—the same as the *gematria* of the word *ratzon*, which refers to Hashem's Will. The idea being that the specific name of Hashem that is being revealed reflects upon how Hashem chooses to relate to the world at that point—His Will. In his statement acknowledging his overwhelming *tzaros*, Yaakov referred to the name of Hashem of *Shakai*. Chazal teach us that this name refers to the fact that "*she'amar l'olamo dai*"—Hashem told His world to cease from its expansion. The world was expanding from its initial creation of "*yesh m'ayin*—something from absolute nothingness," until Hashem commanded it to stop and exist within

2 Ibid., 27:1.
3 Ibid., 47:9.

the dimension that had been created to that point. At a basic level, Hashem had told the world, "*Dai*—Enough!" and that was the essence of Yaakov's *tefillah*. But perhaps there lies a deeper idea within Yaakov's words to Yehudah.

An *adam gadol* once explained that when Hashem said "Enough" to the expanding universe, He did this so that it would still be possible for His Presence to be recognized in the world. As the *Maharal* explains in many places, the more complex and diverse the world becomes, the harder it is to perceive the One Creator. The world was expanding to great dimensions, and Hashem decreed, "*Dai*!" Had the world expanded any further, the capacity for Man to sense Hashem's Presence would have been compromised. Thus, Hashem said, "*Dai*."

The world is called *olam*, which means "hidden." Hashem's Presence in His world must be hidden, for if it were to be openly revealed, then the purpose of creation could not be accomplished. Man, through his *bechirah* to choose between good and evil, must *work* to believe in the Creator, and there lies his capacity to be rewarded in *Olam Haba*. By earning his reward through his *avodah* with *bechirah*, he can be legitimately considered the true bearer of his reward for eternity. This is why a sense of balance had to be created. Hashem had to be present in the *olam*, but He would have to be *ne'elam*, hidden. He would not be hidden to the point that He couldn't be found, but to the point necessary to establish a valid sense of *bechirah*. For this reason, when the world was expanding to the point where Man wouldn't be able to *find* the Creator, Hashem said, "*Dai*."

A similar situation occurred with Yaakov. The challenges he had to bear were necessary to develop his inner potential and bring it to fruition. Yaakov was most certainly not complaining about the darkness of his life. When he compared his troubles to Hashem's command of *Dai*, he was saying that he was at the end of his ability to maintain the correct perspective. He prayed that *Dai* should be said to his *tzaros* because he feared that were he to experience any more, they might destroy him—he might no longer be able to perceive Hashem's light in the midst of unbearable darkness. His words, therefore, represented his *tefillah* that Hashem should say *Dai* to his *tzaros* so he would be able to continue to recognize Hashem's Hidden Presence in creation. Chazal reveal that Eisav's ultimate downfall will be through the children of Rachel: Yosef, and when Yosef is gone, it is Binyamin who takes his place. Through Binyamin it was as if Yaakov had the spiritual *ko'ach* of Rachel and Yosef. Thus, he greatly feared what would be if he lost his precious Binyamin.

We see a similar idea when Yaakov fought the *Saro shel Eisav*, the guardian angel of Eisav, in *Parashas Vayishlach*. The *pasuk* says: "Yaakov was left alone, and a man wrestled with him until daybreak."[4] Chazal explain that the *Saro shel Eisav* served as Eisav's guardian angel, representing the side of evil. If the *Saro shel Eisav* would have been asked whether he wanted to win or lose his battle with Yaakov, he would have said that he wanted Yaakov to overcome him. The *Saro shel Eisav* is a *malach*, angel, and it is his sacred job to serve Hashem by representing Eisav. As a representative of *ra*, evil, his *avodah* is to challenge *tov* to the best of his ability and then hope to be overcome. He couldn't fight Yaakov in a casual way, allowing Yaakov to win, for that wouldn't have accomplished the desired goal. The purpose of his battle was to be a *keli*, vessel, to catapult Yaakov to higher levels of *kedushah*. By challenging Yaakov, he forced him to delve deep within himself and realize the enormous spiritual potential contained within him; without a challenge, this could not be revealed. Thus, the *Saro shel Eisav* directly caused Yaakov's *kedushah* to be revealed. This represents the true meaning of *tzaros*: it is through those very challenges that we are able to grow spiritually.

The lives of the Avos parallel the destiny of Klal Yisrael. Yaakov's *tzaros* represent the history of Klal Yisrael's afflictions. Our history has had many difficult moments.

But the *Maharal* reveals to us an amazing insight. Klal Yisrael's spiritual quest doesn't end with *galus*. When Mashiach comes, the world will be brought to its ultimate state; the entire *briah* will experience light and recognize that "*ein od Milvado*"—there is nothing else but the absolute truth of Hashem. This will be followed by *Olam Haba*, where Klal

---

4 *Bereishis* 32:25.

Yisrael will exist with the truth they acquired through a life of *avodah* in the world of *bechirah*.

The *Maharal* asks where this is represented in the lives of the Avos. He explains that as Chazal teach us, the *pasuk* states: "Yaakov completed his commands to his sons, and he gathered up his feet, to the bed. He expired and was gathered to his people."[5] The *pasuk* tells us about Yaakov, "*vayigva,*" that he expired, but does not mention death, for "*Yaakov Avinu lo meis*—Our father Yaakov did not die."[6] The ultimate end of Klal Yisrael is represented in Yaakov, in the sense that he doesn't die but continues to exist. Klal Yisrael will also be in the realm of "*lo meis,*" because they will continue to exist for all eternity, cleaving to Hashem. The *tzaros* of Klal Yisrael cleanse us, for they come from Hashem, Whom the Gemara refers to as "*Rachmana,*" the One who loves us. May we truly be worthy of His enormous *ahavah* and soon hear in our days His proclamation of "*Dai*" to our *tzaros*.

Everything that occurs to a person is a decree from Hashem. This statement is surely true regarding the many tragedies that occurred during the lives of the Avos:

- Yaakov's brother Eisav sought to kill him, his daughter Dinah was attacked by Shechem, and his precious son Yosef was lost to him for all those many years.
- Yitzchak became blind.
- Nimrod wanted to kill Avraham, and his wife did not give birth to Yitzchak until he was one hundred years old.

These, as well as other incidents, are part of the spiritual destiny of the Avos and of Klal Yisrael. There is a basic pattern to the major moments of their lives. It represents the *yesod* of "*maaseh avos siman l'banim,*" that which occurred to the Avos prepared the path for their future generations.

---

5 Ibid., 49:33.

6 *Masechta Taanis* 5b.

The *Maharal* in *Derech Chaim* explains that Avraham, Yitzchak, and Yaakov planted spiritual *kochos* and qualities into the souls of their children, Klal Yisrael. "*Maaseh avos siman l'banim*" applies not only with regard to individual occurrences, such as when Avraham prayed in Shechem for Yaakov's children who would eventually wage war against the city to save their sister Dinah, but also to the fate of the entire nation. The *Maharal* reveals to us that the complete destiny of Klal Yisrael is mirrored within the lives of Avraham, Yitzchak, and Yaakov.

AVRAHAM AVINU

Avraham Avinu was the first of the Avos, and his life therefore parallels the beginning of Klal Yisrael. He was oppressed by Nimrod and eventually thrown into the fiery furnace, where Nimrod attempted to kill him. However, from the time Hashem revealed Himself to Avraham, his life was transformed into one of a more tranquil nature. In *Parashas Lech Lecha* the *pasuk* says: "The King of Sodom went out to meet him [Avraham] after his return from defeating Kedarlaomer and the kings that were with him, to the Valley of Shaveh, which is the Valley of the King."[7] *Rashi* cites the midrash that explains why this place was known as the Valley of the King. It was here that all the nations gathered together and appointed Avraham over them as a prince of G-d and leader. He was recognized as a great and holy person and lived a life of relative peace.

The *Maharal* explains that this corresponds to the early stages of Klal Yisrael, when they were oppressed by the people of Mitzrayim and were slaves in their land. When Avraham was thrown into the fiery furnace, it served as the "*maaseh avos siman l'banim*" for the time in the future when the babies of B'nei Yisrael would be thrown into the river. From the time of their redemption from Mitzrayim, and their eventual acquisition of Eretz Yisrael, their collective life was as a nation in their own land. This culminated with the building of the first Beis Hamikdash in the times of Shlomo HaMelech, who was recognized as a world leader, with Yerushalayim as his capital. Hashem revealed to Avraham the future redemption from Mitzrayim, as the *pasuk* says: "And Hashem said

---

7 *Bereishis* 14:17.

to Avram, 'Know for sure that your descendants will be aliens in a land that is not theirs. They will enslave them and oppress them for four hundred years. But also, that nation whom they will serve I will judge; afterward, they will leave with great wealth.'"[8] *Geulas Mitzrayim* refers to the beginning of Klal Yisrael and was therefore within the realm of Avraham Avinu. This explains why the end of the life of Avraham is described as: "Avraham expired and died *b'seivah tovah*, in a good old age, old and satisfied."[9] He represented the starting point of Klal Yisrael.

YITZCHAK AVINU

The life of Yitzchak was one of sorrow, as the midrash says: "*Yitzchak chidash yesurin*—Yitzchak initiated suffering."[10] Prior to the *Akeidah*, when he was almost offered as a sacrifice to Hashem by his father, Avraham, he had no wife,[11] and from that time on, he progressively became blind. His eventual blindness and lack of personal light parallels the intermediate stage of Klal Yisrael, when the Beis Hamikdash was destroyed and its *ohr* was extinguished. Yitzchak's life thus depicted the unfortunate stature of Klal Yisrael in their time of *churban*. No *geulah* was revealed to him, for his life was to represent destruction.

In discussing the life and death of Yitzchak, the *pasuk* in *Parashas Vayishlach* states: "Yitzchak's days were one hundred and eighty years. And Yitzchak expired and died."[12] The *pasuk* clearly references the fact that Yitzchak died, and unlike Avraham and Yaakov, it doesn't say that he **lived** for a certain amount of years; merely that his days were one hundred and eighty years.

The *Ohr Hachaim* writes that until the *Akeidah*, when he was bound upon the altar by his father Avraham in preparation for being slaughtered as a *korban*, Yitzchak was not yet married. Chazal say that one who lives without a wife has no *chayim*, life. Then, from the time of the *Akeidah*, Yitzchak's eyesight began deteriorating, and as Chazal explain,

---

8 Ibid., 15:13.

9 Ibid., 25:8.

10 *Bereishis Rabbah*, *parashah* 65:9.

11 As it says in *Koheles Rabbah* (*perek* 9), "One who lives without a wife is as if he isn't alive."

12 *Bereishis* 35:28–29.

a blind person is considered as a *meis*, one who is not alive. But perhaps the most revealing statement of Chazal is based upon the words of the *Tochachah* in *Parashas Bechukosai*: "I will remember My covenant with Yaakov and also My covenant with Yitzchak, and also My covenant with Avraham I will remember."[13] Chazal point out that *zechirah*, Hashem's remembrance of His covenant with the Avos, is mentioned with regard to Yaakov and Avraham. Yet, when Hashem speaks regarding His covenant with Yitzchak, the *pasuk* says: "And also My covenant with Yitzchak," omitting mention of remembrance. Chazal explain that there is no need to reference remembrance with regard to Yitzchak because "Yitzchak's ashes are heaped in a mound upon the *Mizbei'ach*," the Altar, and thereby clearly seen.[14] The presence of Yitzchak's *mesiras nefesh* is always before Hashem, for indeed, his ashes are visible atop the *Mizbei'ach*. Thus, although Yitzchak was what we would call being alive, in some sense, he was considered actually as one who wasn't, and it was this lack of existence that parallels the years when Klal Yisrael "lived" within the state of *churban*.

YAAKOV AVINU

The beginning years of Yaakov were ones of sorrow and tragedy. He fled from the evil Eisav, battled with the sly Lavan, suffered the *tzarah* of Dinah, and mourned the seeming loss of his precious son Yosef. In *Parashas Vayigash*, Yaakov meets Pharaoh and tells him: "The years of my temporary residence are one hundred and thirty years. Few and troublesome have been the days of my life."[15] Yaakov prayed to "*Keil Shakai*"—that He Who said "Enough" to the ever-increasing world, should please say "Enough" to his tragedies. Although it is true that until his coming to Mitzrayim he suffered much pain, his life from then on was beyond merely peaceful. He existed in a relative state of bliss and experienced a sense of *Olam Haba* while yet still on this world. His life was transformed from its early tragic elements to one of absolute peace

---

13 *Vayikra* 26:42.

14 *Vayikra Rabbah* 36:5.

15 *Bereishis* 47:9.

and tranquility. The *pasuk* in *Parashas Vayechi* states: "Yaakov called for his sons and said, 'Assemble around, and I will tell you what will happen to you in the End of Days.'"[16] Yaakov wished to reveal to them the ultimate *geulah* from the final *galus* that we are living through today. Hashem revealed this secret to Yaakov because he represents the great endpoint and future destiny of Klal Yisrael. The tragic beginning of his life corresponds to the times of *galus* that his children would suffer, but the total peaceful end of his life parallels the great future that his children will be *zocheh* to in the world of Mashiach and of *Olam Haba*.

Therefore, the different life circumstances that the Avos were subjected to represent "*maaseh avos siman l'banim*" and how they established the way for their children to arrive at *Acharis HaYamim*. The three Avos experienced different life events because these portended the three basic *zemanim* in the great history of their children, Klal Yisrael.

We have seen the cycles of light and darkness, tranquility and suffering, that affected the Avos throughout their history and Am Yisrael throughout all of history.

The *pasuk* in *Parashas Vayeilech* states: "And now, write this song for yourselves, and teach it to B'nei Yisrael, place it in their mouth, so that this song shall be for Me a witness against B'nei Yisrael."[17] *Rashi* explains that the song referred to is that of the next *parashah*, "*Haazinu ha'shamayim*—Give ear the heavens."[18] The word *shirah*, song, is an expression of happiness and the result of a heart overflowing with joy. Yet, in this *shirah*, punishments are present that should seemingly remove its capacity to be a true song. Nevertheless, it is still referred to as a *shirah*, and the *Sefas Emes* gleans a profound *yesod* regarding the punishments Klal Yisrael may experience en route to *Acharis HaYamim*.

The *pasuk* in *Parashas Pinchas* that deals with the *korban Mussaf* of Rosh Hashanah states: "The first day of the seventh month shall be a sacred holiday to you when you should not do any work of consequence.

---

16 Ibid., 49:1.

17 *Devarim* 31:19.

18 Ibid., 32:1.

It shall be a *yom teruah*, a day of sounding of the ram's horn."[19] The word "*teruah*" here is the same word used in *Parashas Balak*, where the *pasuk* says: "He does not see evildoers in Yaakov; and He has seen no transgression in Yisrael; Hashem, his G-d, is with him, *u'teruas melech bo*, and he has the King's friendship."[20] *Rashi* explains that the word *teruah* stems from the word *rei'us*, friendship and love. This is surprising because we are all well aware of the fear that permeates throughout all Klal Yisrael on the *Yom Ha'din*.

The *Sefas Emes* explains that punishment and *tzaros* are not meant to hurt, *chalilah*, but rather to inspire and cleanse. What we, as individuals or a *tzibbur*, endure is meant to awaken us up from our slumber of living in *Olam Hazeh* in our comfortable and set ways. Through what we receive from Hashem, we are brought to recognize that there is *din*, justice, and a *Dayan*, Hashem, Who judges and metes out justice. The Torah discusses the punishment of *malkus*, the thirty-nine lashes given due to transgressing basic prohibitions of the Torah. The *pasuk* says: "*V'niklah achicha*—And your **brother** will be lessened in your eyes,"[21] meaning that once the person is lashed as punishment for his sin, he then becomes *achicha*, your brother. This is because the punishment he was subjected to cleansed his soul and gave him the ability to return to the proper path of *avodas Hashem*. Therefore, even on the *Yom Ha'din* of Rosh Hashanah, the sounding of the shofar is meant to awaken the connection we are fortunate to have with our Creator.

These words of the *Sefas Emes* are a beacon of light amid the darkness of Jewish history in *Olam Hazeh*: they are truth. The challenge is how we will incorporate this most profound idea into the basic fiber of our lives. The Gemara in *Masechta Berachos*[22] may shed light on how we may realize this ideal.

The Gemara says that on good tidings, one recites the blessing of "*HaTov U'Meitiv*," that Hashem is good and does good, and the blessing

---

19 *Bamidbar* 29:1.

20 Ibid., 23:21.

21 *Devarim* 25:3.

22 60b.

of "*Dayan Emes*," that Hashem is the true Judge, on bad tidings. But Rava adds a requirement to the blessing of *Dayan Emes*: we are to accept the bad tidings as we accept the good. *Rashi* adds another dimension to this point. We are to recite the *berachah* of *Dayan Emes b'leivav shalem*, with a complete and full heart. Perhaps here lies the key for mortal man living in *Olam Hazeh* to accept the difficulties they endure in the most positive of ways.

We live within the physical confines of the mundane world of *Olam Hazeh*. But we also possess a certain capacity to soar beyond the physical and the "now," and to dwell in the spiritual realm of *Olam Haba*. The heart of Man is just such a *keli*, and through it we can sense the world of spirituality beyond. The heart pumps vitality into the very existence of the person and can be considered as responsible for the life the person experiences. In this vein, it is similar to the realm of *Olam Haba*, which pumps "life" into the mundane world of *Olam Hazeh*. The purpose of our presence in the world is that through our *avodah* here, we earn our right to exist in the world of reward of *Olam Haba*. Thus, both the heart and *Olam Haba* share the function of giving life.

Rav Tzadok in *Takanas Ha'shavin* (*perek* 3), in the name of Chazal, says that the heart is "*sod almah d'asi*—the mystery and secret of the World to Come." It is true that we are not able to verbalize the *berachah* of *HaTov U'Meitiv* on a tragedy. However, the same person who cannot legitimately recite those words on tragedy must strive to appreciate them in the hidden *keli* that enables his connection to *Olam Haba*—his heart. Within our hearts lies our ability to accept what Hashem places upon us—whether we are able to perceive it as good and verbalize it as such or not.

It is for this reason that the Torah refers to the words of *Parashas Haazinu* as a *shirah*. All is good, whether we are able to actively recognize it or not. When we do, we can easily sing, but when the darkness we experience challenges our ability to raise our voices to Hashem, a different form of song is required. Then our hearts must rise to the microphone, to quietly proclaim that there is no evil that emanates from Heaven. This is how we are to understand the concept of punishment.

There is yet an additional aspect as to how the heart relates to the ultimate good. One of the most haunting questions that challenge each of us is whether we are sincere in our *avodas Hashem*. Since the sin of Adam HaRishon, the world is a mixture of *tov* and *ra*. One performs mitzvos, but their motive may not always be purely to serve Hashem; it may be to acquire fame or the like. What are our hearts made of? Rav Yitzchak Isaac Chaver writes that there is a way for a person to perceive what is truly buried in his heart. The *gematria* of *lev*, heart, is thirty-two, equal to that of *bechi*, the crying of tears. If a person is moved to tears upon gazing at a sunset, he has glimpsed a little of what is buried deep within him. But if he cries on Yom Kippur because he seeks G-d, this demonstrates that alive in his heart is his burning desire to be *davak b'Hashem*. Tears cannot be faked, and they reveal what we truly are. The world of *Olam Haba* is one of absolute truth, and there one will receive exactly what he has earned through his *avodah* in this world. Therefore, both the heart of Man and the World to Come stand for absolute truth.

The *pasuk* in *Parashas Mikeitz* states: "And it came to pass at the end of two full years that Pharaoh dreamed, and behold he was standing by the river."[23] So began the rise of Yosef, from being a prisoner in the dungeons of Mitzrayim to become the viceroy and second-in-command of that very land. Nothing happens by chance, and the fact that Yosef had to suffer for many years as a slave must also be meaningful. We have seen that darkness precedes light, and that difficulties are designed by Hashem for our benefit. How can we understand why it took all those years until the Torah states the words, "Pharaoh dreamed," which preceded the promotion of Yosef? In other words, while we can understand the need for difficulties in order to grow, why do our troubles seem to encompass many years of our lives, and why have Am Yisrael's troubles lasted millennia?

The *Maharal* in *Gevuros Hashem* deals with this issue. He refers to a similar question when dealing with the initial development of the

---

23 *Bereishis* 41:1.

nation of Klal Yisrael. From the actual moment when the *shivim nefesh*, the seventy souls, went down with Yaakov and entered the gates of Mitzrayim until they were redeemed and became a nation was two hundred and ten years. Why couldn't it have happened right away—or at least in a shorter period of time? The *Maharal* explains that in the natural, physical world, those elements that are meant to develop spiritual qualities require a complex developmental process. The *Maharal* in *Tiferes Yisrael* discusses the birth of a child as opposed to that of an animal:

- When an animal such as a horse is born, within moments it is able to run and act as a horse is designed to do.
- A human child is born incapable of fending for itself. If the infant's parents would not be actively involved, the child would not be able to survive.

This is a curious anomaly. Man is the purpose of existence and its central figure, so why is he so vulnerable? But here lies the key. The fact that Man is the focal point of all that Hashem created establishes his need to develop. The physical framework of our world is in accordance with elements that are physical. With Man's spiritual soul comes the need for that identity to develop within this world. The higher the destiny of a particular creation, the more time is necessary to establish it. While the horse can function as a horse immediately, for that is what it will always remain, a human must develop since he is destined for spiritual greatness. He is not a physical entity that is enabled right away, but is rather a spiritual entity—and the spirit needs time. We can now understand why Klal Yisrael was the last of the nations that were created.

The seventy nations were established as a result of the *dor ha'flagah*, the generation that built a tower and planned to battle against Hashem. While they were a united people, it was this unity that fostered their desire to rebel. Their punishment was that they were scattered all over the world and broken up into seventy nations. The nations of Amon and Moav were created later, as well as those of the children of Yishmael and Eisav. Klal Yisrael, however, came into being at *krias Yam Suf* and were thus the last of the nations. The *Maharal* explains that the nations serve the role of *chomer*, physical matter, while Klal Yisrael serves the role as their *tzurah*, the "definer" that cultivates their spiritual sense of purpose and identity to which they should aspire. The *Maharal* explains that whatever occurred to B'nei Yisrael during their sojourn in Mitzrayim mirrors what happened to Yosef when he was in Mitzrayim.

Mitzrayim is to be understood as the *chomer*, the most physical and earthy of the nations. They were the most immoral and thus totally dedicated to their physical existence. It was Yosef who became the viceroy and leader of such a nation because it is ultimately the power of the *tzurah* to govern over and be in charge of the *chomer*. But such a process takes time. The development of the spiritual *tzurah* is the slow process by which physical mass gains its spiritual dimension. A child cannot speak when born, for his spirituality is totally dominated by his physical identity. As he matures and his spiritual self, his *daas*, begins to take shape, he gains the capacity to speak. Thus, when Yosef entered the land of Mitzrayim, the building process began because he was to be the *mashbir*, the one who pumps life and meaning into the most physical of all lands, Mitzrayim. This is a process that requires time.

This is a very important aspect for a *ben Torah* to appreciate. We try, yet sometimes we fail, and then we sense feelings of frustration that might cause us to give up our quest of attaining our spiritual destiny. But we can't allow ourselves to fall prey to such feelings. The human needs more time to develop than the animal. More so, the *ben Torah* needs more time than the mere human. The true *ben Torah* is the person for whom Hashem proclaimed, "*Naaseh Adam*,"[24] and he must therefore realize that time and patience are required to create this choicest of beings. May we be *zocheh* to remember this vital point that we learn from the emergence of Yosef HaTzaddik.

---

24 Ibid., 1:26.

Suffering

THE PASUK TOWARD the end of *Parashas Shemos* states: "*U'me'az basi el Pharaoh...*—From the time I came to Pharaoh to speak in Your name, he did evil to this people."[1] Moshe was sent from Hashem to serve as the *go'el*, redeemer, of B'nei Yisrael, yet from the time he came before Pharaoh representing B'nei Yisrael, Pharaoh increased the burden of their *shibud*. When Moshe said this to Hashem, he was told: "Now you will see what I shall do to Pharaoh."[2] To understand the reason for the increased bondage, as well as Hashem's subsequent response, we must discuss the meaning of the *shibud* itself.

What occurred in Mitzrayim was based upon the events that had transpired years before at the beginning of creation, in Gan Eden between the *nachash* and Adam and Chavah. The words that seem to introduce the entire episode of the *cheit* of Adam HaRishon were: "They were both *arumim*—naked, the man and his wife."[3] Immediately after that statement, the next *pasuk* begins with the *nachash* planning his attack on Adam and Chavah with the words: "Now the serpent was *arum*—cunning."[4] Chazal reveal that the external reason why the *nachash* planned his attack was based upon his desire for Chavah—the *pasuk* referring to the cunningness of the *nachash* as "*arum*" is connected to the fact

1 *Shemos* 5:23.

2 Ibid., 6:1.

3 *Bereishis* 2:25.

4 Ibid., 3:1.

that Adam and Chavah were *arumim*. As a result of the *cheit* of Adam eating from the *Eitz Ha'daas*, evil was implanted within the *etzem tzuras adam*, the basic human structure. In order for the goal of the *briah* to be realized, the resulting *zuhamah*, spiritual poison, had to be cleansed. B'nei Yisrael had to therefore go down to the land of Mitzrayim to begin the *shibud* that was meant to spiritually cleanse them.

Twice each day, we end off the third *parashah* of *Krias Shema* with the words, "I am Hashem, your G-d, Who has removed you from the land of Mitzrayim to be a G-d to you." The *Ramchal*, in his *sefer Derech Hashem*, explains that we say these words, for they represent the reason that we are *zocheh* to be privy to the relationship with Hashem for eternity. All mankind was initially included within Adam HaRishon, and so when he sinned, all mankind was subject to catastrophic spiritual decline. Avraham, Yitzchak, and Yaakov developed their souls to be free of the spiritual poison of the *nachash*, and as a result, their children are intrinsically different than any other people on the face of the earth. During the *Bris Bein Habesarim*, the covenant Hashem made with Avraham in *Parashas Lech Lecha*, Hashem decreed: "*Ger yihyeh zarecha*"[5]—your descendants will be foreigners in a land that is not theirs and they will be enslaved and oppressed. This enslavement in Mitzrayim would complete the cleansing process that had begun with the Avos and would enable B'nei Yisrael to stand at Har Sinai with the spiritual status of "*paskah zuhamah shel nachash*"—the *nachash*'s spiritual poison would cease with regard to B'nei Yisrael.[6]

This process is also reflected in the words of the Pesach Haggadah. Yaakov and Eisav were both descendants of Yitzchak Avinu. The *mesorah* of the blessings of the Avos was given to Yaakov, for his children were to fulfill the spiritual destiny that they had begun. As the *Baal Haggadah* writes in the paragraph beginning, "*Mi'techilah ovdei avodah zarah*—Originally our fathers were idolaters," it ends with the words, "And I [Hashem] gave to Yitzchak, Yaakov and Eisav, and I gave to Eisav Har Se'ir to inherit it, while Yaakov and his children went down

---

5 *Bereishis* 15:13.
6 *Masechta Yevamos* 103b.

to Mitzrayim." Eisav was given his share in this world at that time, while Yaakov and his children would inherit the spiritual destiny that required the *shibud* of Mitzrayim to cleanse them of any impropriety. The *Shelah HaKadosh* in *Parashas Shemos* discusses interesting parallels between the *shibud* of Mitzrayim and the *cheit* of Adam HaRishon.

The *pasuk* in *Yechezkel* refers to Pharaoh as "*Ha'tanim ha'gadol*—the great serpent,"[7] for he represented the process of the *shibud* that would cleanse the *cheit* instigated by the original serpent. The first miracle performed by Moshe was with a snake, as the *pasuk* in *Parashas Va'eira* says: "Take your staff and throw it down before Pharaoh; it will become a snake."[8] Pharaoh represented the *nachash* in his confrontation with Moshe, while Moshe sought to control the power of the *nachash* and subjugate it under the dominion of *kedushah*. The *shibud* of Mitzrayim was meant to cleanse the emerging nation of Klal Yisrael, and when the level was increased, it meant that a higher level was needed to accomplish the purge. Therefore, it was after the bondage was increased that Hashem told Moshe, "Now you will see what I shall do to Pharaoh." Growth emerges from *he'edar*, the absence of perfection and true sense of existence. The greater the *shibud*, the greater the ultimate spiritual growth, for such is the remedy of *shibud*.

With this background, we can perhaps better understand why the Jewish nation—Hashem's nation—seems to have suffered more than any other nation in the world. The *Maharal* in *Netzach Yisrael* agrees with this statement and reveals insightful ideas regarding this issue. The discussion here is not meant to explain specific tragedies that have befallen us but aims to provide a framework and an overall view with which to approach them.

Within the actual building blocks of the *kedushah* of Klal Yisrael, we find *nissim*, miracles. One could assume that these glimpses of the cessation of natural law are the instances in which B'nei Yisrael were

7 *Yechezkel* 29:3.

8 *Shemos* 7:9.

fortunate to be saved from calamity or destruction, but this approach would not only be merely superficial; it would be incorrect. The *Maharal* reveals that we are not merely subject to these miracles; they define us for what we truly are. Rav Yitzchak Isaac Chaver explains this point in his *Haggadah Yad Mitzrayim.*

Avraham Avinu was confronted by the evil Nimrod and was challenged to either forfeit his belief in One G-d or be thrown into the fiery furnace. Avraham stood fast and refused to disavow his belief in Hashem. Nimrod threw him in, but Avraham emerged unscathed.

This is surprising, for these are not the rules of the physical world we live in. Within the framework of *Olam Hazeh*, Avraham should have died. Rav Yitzchak Isaac Chaver writes that, in a sense, he did. The fact that he survived was because his sense of being and true identity were at that moment established as existing not for the mundane physical world of *Olam Hazeh*, but as totally associated with the world of pure *kedushah* of *Olam Haba*.

The birth of Yitzchak represented the next step in the creation of an entire nation bearing this identity. Chazal reveal to us that it wasn't merely that Sarah experienced problems in conceiving Yitzchak; she actually lacked the physical elements necessary to have a child. Once again, within the framework of *Olam Hazeh*, it would have been impossible for Yitzchak to be born. But the fact that he *was* born established the future Klal Yisrael as a nation that isn't subject to the restraints of natural law. Their being subject to *nissim* defines them as a different species of Man than the rest of the people of the world.

The climax of the creation of this holy nation occurred during *yetzias Mitzrayim* at *krias Yam Suf*. B'nei Yisrael were faced with certain destruction. There were Egyptians behind them and the waters of the sea in front of them. Within the framework of the rules of *Olam Hazeh*, people cannot walk in the sea. But they did, for it split and allowed them to walk through. Once again, the rules and regulations of the world were unique to them. Human beings would die in such a situation, but B'nei Yisrael not only survived—Chazal teach us that they flourished at that point as a result of all the miracles that occurred to them.

The *Maharal* is teaching us that we, Klal Yisrael, are not normal and simple human beings. Regular people live in this world within the guidelines of a physical existence:

- When Avraham was thrown into the fiey furnace, he was considered to have died a physical death within the framework of *Olam Hazeh*.
- In terms of the physical world, Yitzchak could not have been born.
- In terms of *Olam Hazeh*, Klal Yisrael cannot walk in the sea. But they did, because their existence was being established in terms of *Olam Haba*.

It is this point that is the key: we do not and *cannot* live within the rules of *Olam Hazeh*. Therefore, when we sin and attempt to shed our spiritual identity of striving for *Olam Haba*, we lose our ability to survive. In the terms of this world, we don't exist. Thus, when we forget what we are and purely live in terms of a physical existence, we cease to exist. It is through the mercy of Hashem that we are able to survive to wake up to a spiritual next day, but theoretically, at the moment we sin, we forfeit our true right to exist. The nations of the world live in this world, and even though they may do horrible things, that doesn't counter their right to exist purely within *Olam Hazeh*. Thus, we suffer, for we are subject to an existence in the spiritual realm and not that of the mundane.

Rav Tzadok explains an added point that portrays this concept. Chazal teach us that a non-Jew who keeps Shabbos is obligated to be killed. Rav Tzadok explains that here, too, the idea is that he forfeits *his* existence. A gentile lives purely for the physical realm and is not able to relate to *Olam Haba*. If he keeps Shabbos, he is attempting to connect with the *me'ein Olam Haba*, the glimmer *of Olam Haba* that is inherent in *kedushas Shabbos*. This, for him, is his destruction. The foundation of his world is that he exists as a physical being performing physical acts. When he refrains from such acts on Shabbos, he is negating his very own sense of identity. His world is that of the physical, and without it, he has no existence. Therefore, he ceases when he attempts to relate to *Olam Haba*. Similarly, when we attempt to establish *Olam Hazeh* as our permanent residence, we are subject to the tragedies that we have endured over the years. The suffering is not a function of who we are; it is a result of the awesome potential greatness that is uniquely ours.

This idea also affects another aspect of our lives: *ye'ush*, when we feel defeated and give up. Whatever happens, we must realize that there is no such thing as a "knockout punch" from *Shamayim*. Whatever we are challenged with is something we are able to overcome, for it represents our *avodah*. Rav Tzadok writes that there cannot be any sense of *ye'ush* among any member of B'nei Yisrael. The very foundations of *Yiddishkeit* are built upon the denial of any expression of *ye'ush*. Avraham and Sarah were physically incapable of having a child, yet Yitzchak was nevertheless born. We exist for the world of *Olam Haba* and are not truly subject to the bounds and regulations of the physical world. True, within the dimensions of the physical, we should give up, but that is not our identity, it is not who we are. We must seek the help of Hashem through *tefillah*. If we were truly incapable of overcoming the particular challenge we are facing, Hashem wouldn't have brought it upon us. He doesn't want us to fail; He wants us to apply the full spectrum of our enormous storehouse of spiritual *kochos* and emerge successful in our *avodas Hashem*. So, although it might sound simplistic to say, "Don't give up," it truly is not.

We can now better understand why Am Yisrael suffers so much. Of course, any punishments brought against Klal Yisrael from Hashem are all meant to lead to a positive result. We suffer to either awaken us to do *teshuvah*, to cleanse us from the *aveiros* we have committed, or as *yissurim shel ahavah*, suffering that will enhance our existence in *Olam Haba*. The *Maharal* in *Netzach Yisrael* discusses this point and puts it into context.

The *Maharal* discusses a *yesod* that basically permeates the entire structure of Hashem's world. As mentioned above, Hashem created a framework based upon *chomer*, basic mass, and *tzurah*, the element's specific form and purpose. From mere objects to people and even nations, everything falls within the structure of *chomer* and *tzurah*. We will begin with basic objects and how they are part of this *yesod*.

A desk is composed of wood, metal screws, plastic pieces, and whichever other parts are necessary to make it function as a desk. All of these physical elements—the *chomer*—are required to enable the form and purpose—the *tzurah*—to exist. Without its *tzurah*, the physical parts remain merely physical entities that in no way provide meaning for their own existence. The mass of *chomer* doesn't perform; it serves no purpose. The mere *chomer* thereby relates to the physical world, which on its own has no meaning and purpose. It was into this physical *chomer* that Hashem placed *kedushah*, and it is this aspect that establishes its connection with Hashem and gives it meaning.

Everything Hashem created reflects His *kavod*, honor, in the world. Each element bears its own song, as we see in the words of *Perek Shirah*. Thus, the spiritual quotient of all things lies in its *tzurah*. It is not only with regard to objects that this is true, but in relation to people as well.

Man's body is his *chomer*, while his soul represents his *tzurah*. This quality exists in Man and encompasses nations as well. Although initially, all mankind was meant to relate to Hashem *l'netzach*, for eternity, in *Olam Haba*, this opportunity was lost as a result of Adam's *cheit* by eating of the forbidden fruit of the *Eitz Ha'daas*. The state of *kilkul*, spiritual damage, present within the soul of his children would preclude a direct relationship with Hashem. The Avos cleansed that spiritual blemish in order to establish the roots of a nation that would be spiritually able to relate to Hashem. Thus, their children became the new "Adam" of the *briah*, and the destiny of mankind would be found within them. At that point, Klal Yisrael was established as the *tzurah* of the nations of the world, while the nations of the world would be considered the *chomer*.

The *tzurah* defines and gives meaning to the *chomer*, and that is exactly the role that Klal Yisrael serves to the nations of the world. Because they cannot directly relate to Hashem, their capacity to relate to Him on their level occurs through their service and dedication to Klal Yisrael. The *Ramchal*, in his *Maamar Hachochmah*, explains that in *yemos haMashiach*, the era when all mankind will recognize the *Malchus* of Hashem, Klal Yisrael will directly serve Hashem, while the nations will glean their sense of purpose and meaning through their service to Klal Yisrael. As this is the role that Klal Yisrael serves, this explains why they are subject to the punishments that they have endured.

A *cheit* by one of the members of the nations of the world represents a rebellion against Hashem; but it is mere *chomer* that is defying His *Ratzon*, Will. The sins of Klal Yisrael are of a more profound dimension because they represent not just a sin, but a distortion of the *tzurah* as well. There are two parts to Klal Yisrael's *cheit*. One part is that we are indeed people, so our *cheit* represents a violation in the realm of *chomer*. The second part is that we are also the *tzurah* of the world, so this reality catapults our sins to a far more severe level. The *Maharal* explains that the double *lashon* of "*Nachamu, nachamu ami*—Comfort, comfort My people,"[9] of the haftarah of *Parashas Va'eschanan*, which is read directly after Tishah B'Av, the day that represents Klal Yisrael's suffering throughout their history, expresses this point. Our sin was doubled because it was a rebellion of *chomer* and *tzurah*; thus, the *nechamah*, comfort, we will receive from Hashem will also be doubled. We will ultimately be comforted in all the aspects representing our role of *chomer* and *tzurah* in the world.

This is why we are unique in the severity of our punishments, for the sins that we have committed possess an additional significant quality. Thus, because we are great and reflect greatness, we must recognize that it comes with tremendous responsibility.

Klal Yisrael will be privy to the double *nechamah* of "*Nachamu, nachamu ami*" because the seeds and foundation of our ultimate consolation are based upon the intensity of our suffering. So too, the essence of the redemption we will be privy to is founded upon the bondage we endured as well.

---

9 *Yeshayah* 40:1.

The *pasuk* in *Parashas Shemos* states: "The more the Mitzriyim oppressed him [them], the more B'nei Yisrael increased and spread."[10] The Torah is telling us that the more B'nei Yisrael were subject to the physical oppression of *shibud Mitzrayim*, the more they actually increased and became dominant. This reality portrays the essence of the true nature of Klal Yisrael. We can legitimately assume that this would not have occurred with any other nation of the world. How can we come to an appreciation of how this defines the essence of Hashem's holy nation? The *Maharal*, in his *peirush Derech Chaim* on *Pirkei Avos*, reveals an amazing point.

The Mishnah in *Pirkei Avos* states: "This is the way of Torah: eat bread with salt, and drink water in small measure."[11] *Rashi* explains that the Mishnah is talking to the unfortunate person; even though his diet consists of only bread and water, he must still dedicate himself to *limud haTorah*. But if a person would have wealth, his connection to Torah would in no way be affected. The *Maharal* explains, however, that the words of the Mishnah aren't only meant for the financially unfortunate. The words "*Kach hi darkah shel Torah*—This is the way of Torah," seem to imply an entirely different dimension to that of *Rashi*. The *Maharal* continues to explain the awesome relationship a person is to have with *limud haTorah*.

The *pasuk* in *Parashas Toldos* reveals to us that the relationship Yaakov has with Eisav is one of "*K'asher zeh kum, zeh nofel*—When one will stand, the other will fall."[12] Yaakov and Eisav represent the forces that fight for dominance in the world. Yaakov strives to cultivate spiritual dominance, while Eisav's agenda is exclusively the promotion of the body. We are also told that they have an inverse effect on one another. Tzur—the land of the children of Eisav—and the holy city of Yerushalayim cannot exist together in their perfect state. Rather, when one falls, the other will gain prominence. The determining factor lies in Yerushalayim and the children of Yaakov. If they serve Hashem

---

10 *Shemos* 1:12.

11 *Pirkei Avos* 6:4.

12 *Bereishis* 25:23, *Rashi*.

properly, then Yerushalayim will flourish, and Tzur will flounder. But if, *chalilah*, the opposite occurs, and Klal Yisrael does not serve Hashem the way they should, then Tzur will be built and secure while Hashem's city will suffer. In this framework, Yerushalayim represents the spiritual, and Tzur represents the physical.

A similar relationship exists within a person himself. The body of a person obviously portrays the physical aspect, while his soul relates to his spiritual dimension. Both of these qualities cannot flourish at the same time, just like Yerushalayim and its unholy counterpart Tzur. The *Maharal* explains that the Mishnah is precise in its wording of "*Kach hi.*" If one caters primarily to his body, his soul will be subordinated. Only by serving his soul and granting it supremacy—through providing the body with its basic needs and not indulging it in the fulfillment of all its desires—can a person truly connect and acquire *divrei Torah*. The Mishnah is to be understood as giving the recipe for spiritual success—not merely establishing the need to learn Torah despite financial hardship.

The *Maharal* in his *peirush* on *Masechta Sotah* explains that this is what occurred to Klal Yisrael through their servitude in Mitzrayim. B'nei Yisrael had to endure *shibud Mitzrayim* in order to leave and then be born as a nation with a spiritual essence. Like the inverse relationship between Yaakov and Eisav, Klal Yisrael suffered physically in order to be established as a spiritual people. When they exist with their supreme spiritual quotient, they are victorious and mighty, for then they reap the rewards of their close relationship with Hashem. Thus, the more they were physically oppressed, the more spiritual and powerful they became.

The *Maharal* uses this idea to explain the concept of *yissurim*, the afflictions that people suffer. He writes that when a person suffers in this world, he is establishing that his true core is that of the spirit. Although he seems to walk along in the physical world of *Olam Hazeh* with other men, his true address is the spiritual realm of *Olam Haba*. B'nei Yisrael, who endured the oppressive *shibud Mitzrayim*, were forging just such a dimension in the collective soul of the nation of Klal Yisrael. To that end they suffered, but ultimately, this is what would form them into the nation of Hashem. Mitzrayim served as the *kur ha'barzel*, smelting pot, that created in Klal Yisrael the capacity to relate in a spiritual fashion.

May we be *zocheh* to understand the profound meaning of all that we endure and recognize that deep within it lies the seeds for our collective and personal redemptions.

Troubles, difficulties, and even oppression can indeed lead to greatness. But this does not occur automatically. If one is able to truly embrace his *yissurim*, recognizing their purpose and not allowing them to overtake his life, then by definition, the suffering does not pain him as much. However, this may lead to a problem. If he does not suffer because he has accepted his fate, does that minimize the *kapparah*? Does that require Hashem to increase the *yissurim* until he does feel the pain?

Above, we dealt with the idea that Klal Yisrael seems to suffer more than any of the other nations of the world. We will now attempt to explain this idea with regard to the individual.

The answer to the question would appear to be no. The person would not be required to suffer increased *yissurim* to truly receive his *kapparah*. A comparison can be made in terms of the *sechar* a person receives as a result of his battle with his *yetzer hara*. When Yaakov received his prophecy of the ladder reaching heaven, the *pasuk* in *Parashas Vayeitzei* states: "And behold! Hashem was standing above him, and He said, 'I am Hashem, G-d of Avraham your father, and G-d of Yitzchak.'"[13] Hashem placed His name upon Avraham, who had already died, and upon Yitzchak as well, even though Yitzchak was alive and theoretically subject to the influence of the *yetzer hara*. Yet, later in dealing with the evil Lavan, Yaakov says, "Had not the G-d of my father—the G-d of Avraham—and the fear of Yitzchak been with me, you would surely have now sent me away empty."[14] Knowing that Yitzchak was still alive, Yaakov was fearful to place Hashem's name on him. *Rashi* explains that although Hashem would not place His name upon one who is still

13 Ibid., 28:13.
14 Ibid., 31:42.

alive because he still is a *baal bechirah*, one who has freedom of choice, Yitzchak was blind, and being locked within his house, his *yetzer hara* had ceased from him. Here lies the key to appreciating man's *avodah* to Hashem.

Sefarim explain that Yitzchak's blindness was a function of the greatness of his spiritual stature. His was the world of the *p'nim*, the internal realm of *kedushah*, and it is there that could be considered his true address. While he physically walked here in our realm, his dimension of existence was in terms of his soul. He therefore became blind, for his vision focused on inner spirituality; the mere vision of the external was meaningless to him. His lack of *bechirah* because his *yetzer hara* had ceased was a function of his *avodah*. Since Yitzchak created that spiritual situation, he was able to reap its rewards in terms of the *sechar* he would receive for not committing a *cheit*. When the spiritual status of a person is based upon his own *avodah* and not merely a function of being created that way, he is able to receive *sechar*. The diligent student who trains himself to sit and toil in Torah receives *sechar* as a function of his personal dedication and not merely due to the *teva*, nature, bestowed upon him by Hashem. A similar concept applies in terms of our question as well.

Yissurim have a specific role in the way Hashem deals with us and the ultimate goal that must be accomplished. But if the person learns the *sefarim* that foster his complete faith and trust in Hashem, and through his profound belief is able to wake up each morning and face the challenges that Hashem, in His ultimate *chochmah*, has chosen to place upon him—that is truly a function of his *avodah*. He has created his own perception of reality, which includes the *yissurim* he is receiving from Hashem. In this way, the *yissurim* are reaching their potential, enabling him to fulfill his ultimate spiritual destiny.

Therefore, the person who properly accepts the afflictions he is subjected to accomplishes the goal of those *yissurim*; he does not need them to increase in magnitude. May Hashem soon bring the day when all pain and suffering will cease.

Galus

KLAL YISRAEL WENT to Mitzrayim and suffered there terribly, only to be redeemed and finally become a nation. Other nations didn't go through this. Why did we?

This observation reflects the basic difference between Klal Yisrael and the rest of the nations of the world. Specifically, because we are Hashem's nation, we are subject to a life that contains an alternate process to that of the rest of the world. The seeds were planted long before the Egyptian servitude. It all begins with the way Hashem created His world.

The *pasuk* in *Parashas Bereishis* states: "And there was evening and there was morning, one day."[1] The *Maharal* in *Netzach Yisrael* explains that this quality of first experiencing night, and only after will the light of day emerge, defines the way Hashem relates to His world. Initially, all that exists is darkness, which represents a lesser form of existence. Only after that state of imperfection can the exalted state of light begin. The key to appreciating and perceiving Hashem's Presence in His world is enabled *after* the imperfection of a world without His added input has been recognized. The goal of Man's creation lies in his recognition that the actual source of all that serves as his world comes from Hashem. The first state of darkness is meant to prove this point to him. Before Hashem bestows His *shefa* upon a person, all is dark.

1 Ibid., 1:5.

The *Sefas Emes* adds an additional idea that specifically deals with our question. The *pasuk* toward the beginning of *Parashas Va'eira* says: "And you shall know that I am Hashem your G-d, Who is bringing you out from under the burdens of Mitzrayim."[2] The *pasuk* seems to be telling us that the ultimate goal of what B'nei Yisrael endured was that they should recognize Hashem as the Creator and Source of the *briah*. Yet, we are being told that this knowledge is only possible as a result of Hashem taking them out of Mitzrayim and their *shibud*. But why was it necessary for B'nei Yisrael to first be in bondage in order to ultimately come to the realization that all is Hashem? The *Sefas Emes* explains that there is an element in a person that causes him to consider himself responsible for his own destiny. This constant battle lies in the arena of "*Kochi v'otzem yadi*"—that it is his own power and ability that grants him all the positive things in his life. But such is not truth. A person who sees himself in terms of his own power is to be understood as a reflection of the darkness of *shibud Mitzrayim*. In truth, without Hashem's input, all is "*tohu va'vohu*," vast and absolute nothingness. But the *shibud Mitzrayim* is supposed to bring home the true sense of horror that represents the person's life before Hashem shines His Goodness upon him. It is therefore only after we recognize what our world would look like without Hashem's input that He comes to redeem us. In other words, the only reason our lives do not resemble the terrible conditions of our ancestors in Egypt is because of Hashem bestowing kindness upon us.

Once we truly understand our inability to exist in an exalted state by ourselves, Hashem will bring us to the state that we are yearning for. He wants all to be good for us, but we first have to recognize Who is the True Source.

The nations of the world do not live within this spiritual framework. All mankind was included in the exalted *neshamah* of Adam HaRishon, but when he sinned and ate from the forbidden fruit of the *Eitz Ha'daas*, it resulted in a spiritual catastrophe. The spiritual status of Adam's soul

---

2 *Shemos* 6:7.

was tainted, and it wasn't until Avraham came along that the process of *tikkun*, repair, began. Through the *avodah* of the Avos, the *neshamos* of the members of B'nei Yisrael were cleansed. As mentioned previously, Chazal explain that at Har Sinai, when the nation received the Torah of Hashem, "*paskah zuhamah shel nachash*"—the spiritual poison inflicted into Adam and Chavah by the *nachash* ceased.

This, however, was not the lot of the members of the nations of the world. The goal of their existence is therefore their performance of the Seven Mitzvos of B'nei Noach, the Seven Noachide laws that create the sense of structure for them to live a "normal" life in the physical world of *Olam Hazeh*. Their spiritual destiny does not include the eternal realm of *Olam Haba* to the extent that is to be the ultimate reward of the children of Avraham, Yitzchak, and Yaakov. The *Ramchal* writes in his *sefer Derech Hashem* that in *Olam Haba*, there will be no nation other than Klal Yisrael.[3] The souls of the *chassidei umos ha'olam*, the righteous gentiles, will be allowed to exist, but only as an addition and attachment to Yisrael. They will be secondary to the Jew, just as a garment is secondary to the person that wears it. This will be their lot because of their nature. They are therefore not primed to recognize the profound dimension of Hashem's Presence in His world.

The *Sefas Emes* adds an important point which is vital to the success of a person's *avodah*. The idea that all would be darkness if not for Hashem is not only in terms of what happens to a person in the course of their lives. It includes what occurs in a person's own *bechirah* as well. Even if a person finds himself in a positive situation where he is consistently choosing good over evil, at any moment—in terms of his own ability—he is ripe to fail. The key to *yetzias Mitzrayim* was in the words of "*Pakod yifkod*—Hashem will surely remember us."[4] Rav Tzadok focuses upon the double *lashon* and explains that "*pakod*"—if we remember the Presence of Hashem and bring Him into our lives, then "*yifkod*"—He will be involved and redeem us. Similarly, when we recognize that we need Hashem for our *avodah*, He will help us; it is

3 *Derech Hashem* 2:4:7.
4 *Shemos* 3:18, *Rashi*.

our *bechirah* that brings Hashem in. But if we foolishly think that it is only our own ability that counts, we will be left to the power of our own devices and will be unfortunately subject to spiritual failure and downfall at any point. The *Sefas Emes* quotes the *pasuk* in *Devarim* that says: "In order that you will remember the day of your departure from the land of Mitzrayim all the days of your life."[5] "All the days" includes the times we are attached to Hashem in our *avodah* and feel positive and connected; but even then, our spiritual identity is fragile and prone to failure in terms of our own abilities.

Therefore, unlike the other nations, we had to be subject to the *shibud Mitzrayim* in order to recognize the profound goodness that Hashem in His Kindness grants us every moment of our lives.

The *geulah* from Mitzrayim had to take place *b'chipazon*, quickly, to prevent B'nei Yisrael from sinking to the fiftieth level of *tumah*—for if this would have happened, they would not have been redeemed. As Hashem is the *Kol Yachol*, He is all Powerful and can do whatever He wants to anyone He wants, why would their sinking to the fiftieth level have caused Klal Yisrael to never be redeemed?

The *Rambam* reveals that during B'nei Yisrael's slavery in Mitzrayim, their connection to Avraham Avinu was about to be severed.[6] The Avos had established a specific dimension of *kedushah* into the collective soul of their children, B'nei Yisrael. The *avodah* of the Avos ensured that their children's spiritual soul was far superior to that of the nations of the world, whose souls were still subject to the imperfections resulting from the *cheit* of Adam HaRishon. This soul, which was permeated with spiritual potential that we inherited from the Avos, was the building block for our ability to survive the *shibud Mitzrayim*, and to emerge spiritually able to receive the Torah on Har Sinai fifty days later.

Yet, the spiritual status of B'nei Yisrael was being drastically challenged. Due to the *shibud*, the people began succumbing to the allures of

5 *Devarim* 16:3.
6 *Hilchos Avodas Kochavim*, chap. 1.

the land of Mitzrayim and the internal holy soul of B'nei Yisrael was becoming compromised. Although they had sunk to the forty-ninth level of *tumah*, they were still able to stay connected to the *kedushah* that the Avos had established in them. But were they to sink any lower, they would have severed their connection to the Avos and forfeited the *kedushah* that was to be their destiny. The necessity for *chipazon* was not that if they would have fallen further, they could not have been redeemed; it was that although Hashem could have redeemed them—for He can do anything—had they fallen to the fiftieth level, their connection to the Avos would have been lost. Hashem could have redeemed them, but they would have needed a new process to replace the profound spirituality that had been lost. The *geulah*, therefore, had to be *b'chipazon* in order to ensure that B'nei Yisrael would still be the nation representing the spiritual children of Avraham, Yitzchak, and Yaakov.

The *Zera Shimshon* answers our question in a different fashion. The Gemara in *Masechta Rosh Hashanah*[7] teaches us that Hashem created in His world fifty levels of understanding, and all were given to Moshe except for one, as the *pasuk* in *Tehillim* says: "Yet, You have made him but slightly less than *Elokim* [i.e., "angels," and also the name of Hashem]."[8] The levels of understanding that relate to *kedushah* are paralleled by corresponding levels of *tumah*. Moshe had reached the highest spiritual level attainable by a human being: the forty-ninth level, with the fiftieth representing the Creator—and unattainable by any mere creation.

The *Zera Shimshon* explains that due to this reality, had the redemption not occurred *b'chipazon* and B'nei Yisrael sunk to the fiftieth level of *tumah*, then Moshe, having attained the corresponding forty-ninth level, would not have had the requisite power to lead the nation out of their corrupted spiritual state. Theoretically, the only hope for the nation was through the *avodah* of Moshe as their leader, and if he lacked this ability, the results would have simply been catastrophic, and the nation would have been spiritually lost. Thus, the fact that the *geulah*

---

7 21b.

8 *Tehillim* 8:6.

occurred *b'chipazon* enabled Moshe to continue as their leader and bring about the redemption.

The *Zera Shimshon* adds a truly fascinating point that helps to explain this idea. Even if they had sunk to the fiftieth level, and Moshe wouldn't have been able to redeem them, Hashem could have brought the *geulah* without Moshe. This brings back our question: if they could have been redeemed even without Moshe, why was there a need for *chipazon*?

Chazal explain that Hashem offered Avraham Avinu the choice of how his children should be dealt with if they would sin in the future: exile and being subjected to the rule of the nations, or Gehinnom, the place of metaphysical punishment. "*Avraham birur lo es ha'mal-cheyos*"[9]—Avraham made the choice that if his children sinned, they should be subject to *galus* and the control of the nations as the preferred way for their sins to be forgiven. The *Zera Shimshon* explains that the redemption had to go through Moshe because if Hashem alone would have brought the *geulah*, B'nei Yisrael would never have been able to be subject to bondage again, and this was not the path Avraham Avinu had chosen.

This explains the need for Moshe to be the redeemer. Had Hashem alone taken out the nation from Mitzrayim, it would have been a *geulah* that could never be revoked in any fashion. Klal Yisrael would thereby acquire the identity of being forever free, but if they would sin, the punishment of exile, as chosen by Avraham, would not have been a possible option.

The redemption from *shibud Mitzrayim* therefore had to come about in a way that enabled the visionary plans of Avraham Avinu to take place. This was why it had to be *b'chipazon*: Moshe had to be involved in the redemption of B'nei Yisrael, yet he would not have been able to bring them out of the fiftieth level of *tumah*.

With this background, we can begin to understand why the haftarah of Shabbos Nachamu contains the double expression of "*Nachamu, nachamu.*"

---

9 *Shemos Rabbah* 51:17.

The Shabbos directly after Tishah B'Av is called Shabbos Nachamu, for it is on this Shabbos that we read the haftarah of "*Nachamu nachamu ami*." Yeshayah HaNavi is prophesizing to us about the consolation of Yerushalayim and proclaims to Klal Yisrael that her period of exile has been completed. The double expression of the prophecy reveals the presence of a dual sense of *nechamah*. Together, these provide the intended level of consolation to a grieving nation. To appreciate this point, we have to understand the essence of the destruction that was brought upon Klal Yisrael.

The midrash in *Parashas Bereishis* teaches us that from the beginning of the creation of the world, the *binyan*, building, as well as the *churban*, destruction, of the Beis Hamikdash is alluded to in the Torah. The *pasuk* that begins the Torah states: "In the beginning of Hashem's creating the heavens and earth, the earth was astonishingly empty, with darkness upon the surface of the deep...Hashem said, 'Let there be light,' and there was light."[10]

- "In the beginning of Hashem's creating the heavens and earth" refers to the building of the Beis Hamikdash (both the first and second).
- "When the earth was astonishingly empty, with darkness upon the surface of the deep" refers to the time of destruction, when there will be no Beis Hamikdash in the world.
- "Hashem said, 'Let there be light,' and there was light" refers to the ultimate *tikkun ha'briah*—the building of the Third Beis Hamikdash by Hashem.

The *Maharal* in *Netzach Yisrael* explains that before the world could reach its absolute fulfillment through the *binyan* of the Third Beis Hamikdash, the state of *churban*, utter destruction, had to precede it. The *pasuk* of "Let there be light" is stated only after the *pasuk* of "When the earth was astonishingly empty, with darkness upon the surface of the deep." The *Maharal* explains a profound and complex concept: true growth can only be built upon the negation of the previous level. He

10 *Bereishis* 1:3.

uses this idea to explain the tremendous growth of B'nei Yisrael during their bondage in Mitzrayim.

The *Maharal* in *Gevuros Hashem* teaches us that as long as the level of Klal Yisrael was at *shivim nefesh*, "seventy souls," the growth to the next level of *shishim ribui*, "six hundred thousand," could not be accomplished. Only once the previous level was lost could the tremendous growth of B'nei Yisrael take place. The process works as follows:

- Things that exist in a state of perfection do not grow and develop.
- When something perceives itself as imperfect, it strives to complete itself.

The *ohr* of Hashem was created after the initial darkness, as the *pasuk* states: "There was evening and there was morning, one day." The *ohr* of Hashem is to be perceived as something that is *mashlim*, completes, the sense of imperfection that naturally exists in a created world. The mere fact that something is created and was not in existence prior to that moment portrays its inherent flaw and *chisaron*. The *binyan* of Klal Yisrael began with the Avos, continued until the twelve *Shevatim*, and reached a degree of completion at *shivim nefesh*. Yet, for Klal Yisrael to reach its zenith, it would have to reach the level of *shishim ribui*. Therefore, the semi-complete stage of *shivim nefesh* had to be lost through the death of its components before Klal Yisrael could evolve to their ultimate state of existence. The *shibud Mitzrayim*, which was necessary to build Klal Yisrael into a holy nation of *shishim ribui*, only began after the death of all the seventy souls that came down to Mitzrayim along with Yaakov Avinu. The reason the Torah refers to *churban* is not merely because it occurred, but because the *churban* represented the foundation for the creation of the ultimate *ohr* of the Third Beis Hamikdash, and in this sense, *had* to occur.

Chazal say that when the Babylonians entered the Beis Hamikdash to destroy it, they found the *keruvim*, the golden figures that, in the First Beis Hamikdash, stood in front of the *Aron*, Ark, enveloped one with another. It is known that the physical positioning of the *keruvim* portrayed the status of the relationship between Hashem and Klal Yisrael:

- When B'nei Yisrael were fully performing the *Ratzon Hashem*, the two *keruvim* faced one another.

- When B'nei Yisrael were not serving Hashem properly, the *keruvim* faced away from each other. This showed that at that moment, B'nei Yisrael's relationship with Hashem was strained.

Yet at the moment of *churban*, which represents the ultimate situation of Klal Yisrael not acting according to the *Ratzon Hashem*, the *keruvim* were embracing each other. This seems to defy the miraculous positioning mentioned above, where we would have expected the opposite.

The *Maharal* explains that according to *Midrash Eichah*, the *ko'ach* of Mashiach was born with the destruction of the Beis Hamikdash. He explains that this is the idea of the *keruvim* embracing one another. True, the moment of *churban* was a function of B'nei Yisrael not properly serving their Creator, but it also had another dimension. The *etzem*, the essence of the *churban*, represented the destruction of the state of semi-*sheleimus*, perfection, making way for the ultimate *sheleimus* of the Third Beis Hamikdash to develop. In this sense, the actual *churban* portrays the quality of Hashem loving and nurturing Klal Yisrael to their ultimate state of perfection. Therefore, says the midrash, the *keruvim* were united, and their posture portrayed the true essence of *churban*: destruction in order to ultimately build.

Within this framework, we can understand the double *nechamah* that Klal Yisrael will be awarded. The basic consolation will be ours, for we will be redeemed. But we will experience a deeper sense of consolation, a second *nechamah*, when we truly perceive that the actual *churban* we endured was the vital foundation upon which was built the Third Beis Hamikdash. This is why the *Navi* quoted "*Nachamu*" twice, for Klal Yisrael will be *zocheh* to a double *nechamah*.

There is an additional point that can enhance our feeling of being comforted from the *churbanos* we endured. As previously mentioned, when the Babylonians came into the *Kodesh HaKadoshim*, they were faced with the two *Keruvim* of the *Aron Kodesh* embracing one another. The *Sefas Emes* questions this, as when B'nei Yisrael were not following *Ratzon Hashem*, the *Keruvim* normally turned away from each other. The *Sefas Emes* explains that at the moment of *churban*, Hashem revealed His absolute and unconditional love for Klal Yisrael because He destroyed His Beis Hamikdash and allowed the nation of Klal Yisrael to survive. Instead of annihilating the people, who were the true cause of the problem, Hashem released His wrath on the wood and stones of the Beis Hamikdash. He didn't destroy the nation because we are His and He loves us, and it was the miracle of the *Keruvim* that portrayed this *ahavah*.

We have seen that destruction is necessary for growth. Darkness is necessary for light. Slavery is necessary for freedom.

In the same vein, Chazal reveal to us that it was fitting and proper for Yaakov Avinu to be forced down to Mitzrayim in chains of iron. We know, however, that he went down with *shivim nefesh* because Yosef, in a sense, paved the way for their coming. Their sojourn in Mitzrayim therefore began in a more pleasant manner than it otherwise would have been. We *had* to endure the *shibud Mitzrayim*, but through the *chessed*, kindness, of Hashem, it at least began in an easier fashion.

We must first begin to discuss why the *shibud* had to be. Twice a day in *Krias Shema*, we acknowledge that it was Hashem Who took us out of Mitzrayim and we must therefore serve Him. The *Ramchal*, in his *sefer Derech Hashem*, teaches us that we must constantly recognize—by day and by night—that we were subject to the bondage of Mitzrayim and Hashem redeemed us from there to be His Nation. There are different reasons discussed among the *mefarshim* as to what the specific *cheit* was that actually necessitated our *shibud*. We will discuss what occurred in a general sense, based on the words of the *Ramchal*.

Initially, all mankind was supposed to have a profound bond and connection with the Creator. When Adam and Chavah sinned by eating from the *Eitz Ha'daas*, mankind suffered a catastrophic blow. Adam didn't merely represent himself as an isolated individual; he incorporated all mankind, to the extent that when he sinned, the entire human species was devastated by his *cheit*. Chazal reveal to us that the souls of all people destined to exist were included in his spiritual composition. Adam was created *b'Tzelem Elokim*, in the image of Hashem, and on that lofty spiritual plane, he was primed to relate to Hashem for eternity.

He was given a test: the command not to eat from the forbidden fruit. When Adam ate and violated the *Ratzon Hashem*, his total stature was minimized. His holy soul had been corrupted, and his capacity to relate to Hashem was greatly damaged. Avraham, Yitzchak, and Yaakov began the cleansing that would eventually catapult the spiritual soul of the nation they would create and enable it to connect with Hashem at the level that was intended for Adam HaRishon. Each of the Avos did their part to repair the damage wrought by the *cheit*, each according to their own spiritual quality—Avraham, of *chessed*; Yitzchak, of *yirah*; and Yaakov, a blending of the two. The goal of creation was accomplished through the Avos, but not in the complete sense. All of mankind was meant to relate to Hashem, and so, the Avos fathered Klal Yisrael, a collective, united nation that represents and replaces the original mankind that had been included in Adam HaRishon. Still, as descendants of Adam, they would still need some degree of cleansing.

The *Ramchal* explains that in some sense, the results of the *cheit* of Adam were still present in the future B'nei Yisrael, and to cleanse that *ra*, they had to be subjected to *shibud Mitzrayim*. Hashem had revealed His Will to the Avos that their children would serve as His nation. The growth of this holy nation had developed from three Avos, the twelve *Shevatim*, the *shivim nefesh*, and ultimately to the *shishim ribui*—the point at which they reached six hundred thousand and were redeemed. Chazal refer to the bondage of Mitzrayim as a *kur ha'barzel*, an iron furnace used to smelt away all the impurities from valuable metals such as gold. Any *pesoles*, improper qualities, that existed within the collective soul of B'nei Yisrael were cleansed through what they experienced in the horrors of their *shibud*. The newly cleansed nation was, in a sense, born at *krias Yam Suf*, when the water of the Sea of Reeds split and enabled the emergence of a holy people. Children are born when they emerge from the water that envelopes them when they are present as a fetus within their mother's *rechem*, womb. Here, too, the new "Adam" of the *briah* was born possessing the capacity to exist with the *Tzelem Elokim* that was originally to be the destiny of all men.

This is what is meant by the "chains" we mentioned above in reference to Yaakov Avinu. The *Ratzon Hashem* has to be accomplished as the ultimate destiny of mankind. Had there been no other way for Yaakov to arrive in Mitzrayim, he would have been led down there in chains. But because of the *chessed* of Hashem, Yaakov and the *shivim nefesh* were able to travel to Mitzrayim to begin the *tikkun* of this holy nation as guests of the viceroy of all Mitzrayim. We had to go down to the *kur ha'barzel* to become a people fitting to cleave to Hashem for all eternity.

This also explains why the harshness of the *shibud* didn't begin until all the members of the original *shivim nefesh* had died. There is a major *yesod* here that transcends this specific point and relates to the general process of how Hashem's world develops. The *Maharal* in *Netzach Yisrael* deals with the issues inherent in this idea.

Our starting point lies in the *pasuk* near the beginning of *Parashas Bereishis*. The *pasuk* says: "Hashem called the light day, and the darkness He called night. It became evening and it became morning, one day." The *pasuk* establishes that within the framework of a Jewish day, night precedes the day. The basis for this idea is that Hashem created a world that by definition must be inherently *chosser*, flawed. Only Hashem exists in a state of "*shalem b'chol minei sheleimus*"—absolute perfection. Mere creations are therefore not of a perfect nature; within that framework of imperfection, they are granted existence through which they can develop their inherent potential from "*ko'ach el ha'poel*"—to the realization of that potential in terms of the pseudo-state of *sheleimus* that is possible for them. Thus, night serves to represent the state of *chesorin*, while day and the ensuing light portrays the sense of striving for perfection and its actual acquisition. The day is considered the added dimension from Hashem that, in a sense, comes to enhance and perfect an imperfect world. Thus, the world is considered to be striving for its sense of completion. The *Maharal* adds that this process of growth is subject to its own set of rules.

The progression of night to day, *chesorin* to *sheleimus*, does not happen **despite** the imperfection of the world, but **because** of its imperfection. The only things that can grow are those that exist in a state of imperfection. If they were to exist in a perfect state, they would stop striving. When a seed is planted into the ground, it initially rots, for in order to grow to its desired level of existence—a full-fledged tree bearing fruit—it must first negate its basic sense of existence as a seed. Even though a seed is incomparable to a tree, it has a pseudo-state of *sheleimus* in its identity as a seed. It therefore will not strive higher to become a tree until its alleged first stage of perfection ceases to exist; it first must rot to enable the state of imperfection, and only then will it strive higher. This is the concept that took place with the advent of *shibud Mitzrayim*.

The *binyan* of Klal Yisrael developed in specific stages:

- It went from the state of the three Avos—Avraham, Yitzchak, and Yaakov—until it reached the twelve *Shevatim*, the children of Yaakov.
- Yaakov traveled down from Canaan to Mitzrayim with the *shivim nefesh*, the next stage of Klal Yisrael.
- The *shivim nefesh* served as a pseudo state of *sheleimus* on the march to Klal Yisrael's ultimate degree of perfection, that of *shishim ribui*.

Thus, the Avos, the twelve *Shevatim*, the *shivim nefesh*, and ultimately the *shishim ribui*, all represent the different degrees of *sheleimus* of the *binyan* of Klal Yisrael. The *pasuk* in *Parashas Shemos* says: "But the more the Egyptians oppressed him [B'nei Yisrael], the more they increased and spread."[11] As we mentioned above, *shibud Mitzrayim* served as the *kur Ha'barzel* to smelt away the impurities and create Klal Yisrael as a pure and holy entity. But as long as the pseudo-state of the *sheleimus* of the *shivim nefesh* existed in any way, the *shibud* needed to create the *shishim ribui* could not begin.

Striving for growth can only come from a state of imperfection. Light cannot exist without darkness. *Geulah* cannot occur without *galus*. If the state of *shivim nefesh* would exist—even if only one member of the original group was still alive—the development to the next level couldn't begin. Therefore, the *shibud*—the process of growth to create

---

11 *Shemos* 1:12.

the ultimate *madreigah* of Klal Yisrael of *shishim ribui*—could not begin until the destruction of the pseudo-state that preceded it, that of *shivim nefesh*.

The above helps to explain why the mitzvah of *sippur yetzias Mitzrayim* on Seder night, where we discuss the wonders Hashem performed for us when He took us out of Mitzrayim, involves first acknowledging that our fathers were idol worshippers. Let us explain.

The *Maggid* portion of the Seder begins with the four questions of the *Mah Nishtanah*, and directly after that states: "We were slaves unto Pharaoh and then Hashem brought us out from there." In the discussion of *Maggid*, we add, "Originally, our fathers were idolaters, and now Hashem has brought us close to His service." Chazal refer to this as "*Maschil b'genus u'mesayem b'shevach*"—we begin by discussing that which represents an embarrassment to us and end with that which is praiseworthy.

In a sense, beginning the Seder in the form of a question and answer also reflects this idea of *maschil b'genus u'mesayem b'shevach* because in the state of a question, all is unclear, and with the answer comes the clarity, which is indeed praiseworthy. There are really two parts to the question:

- The mention of our forefathers as idol worshippers
- The general process of *maschil b'genus u'mesayem b'shevach*

The *Zera Shimshon* deals with the first part of this question. He explains that there is a direct need to admit that our forefathers were idol worshippers. He presents a basic question: It is known that the land of Mitzrayim was a spiritually corrupt place and compromised the *kedushah* of the children of Avraham, Yitzchak, and Yaakov. As mentioned previously, Chazal explain that B'nei Yisrael had sunk to the lowest levels of the forty-nine levels of *tumah*, and had Hashem not taken them out exactly at the moment He did, the nation would have been totally disassociated from the Avos. Hashem could have subsequently redeemed them, but they would not have been the bearers of the spiritual inheritance that they were fortunate to be *mekabel* from the Avos.

The *Zera Shimshon* is therefore asking why B'nei Yisrael had to be exiled to that terrible place to begin with and be forced to endure the back-breaking *shibud*, and he answers that it was because their forefathers were idol worshippers, and they therefore had to be spiritually cleansed.

There is no such thing as "it doesn't matter" within the world of souls. When a person fails and sins, his *neshamah* becomes negatively affected, and the result is that a form of spiritual barrier now exists between the person and Hashem. The results of the *cheit* must be removed to enable the bond between Man and his Creator to exist. The *shibud Mitzrayim* served that role and was necessary due to the forefathers of B'nei Yisrael worshipping *avodah zarah*. They had to be cleansed, and as a result, various situations occurred that ultimately led to their bondage in the land of Mitzrayim.

The *Maharal*, in the beginning of his *sefer Netzach Yisrael*, adds an additional dimension to this idea, relating to the second part of the question. The process of the actual physical world, as well as that which occurs within Man, is a function of growth from a state of imperfection to a state of perfection, through the added Presence of Hashem. The *pasuk* in the beginning of *Parashas Bereishis* states: "And there was evening and there was morning, one day." The makeup of a halachic Jewish day is that first exists the emptiness of the night, which lacks the capacity for true functioning, and only then comes the light of day and all the opportunities that are then possible. This progression reflects the idea that all is lacking until Hashem invests His Presence and spiritual growth can occur. This definition of day mirrors the development of the *kedushah* of Hashem's nation too.

The exalted state of Klal Yisrael could not exist from the moment of its inception. They, too, had to develop from their state of lacking to a state that serves the role of revealing Hashem's Presence in His world. The world is *chosser* and does not initially exist in the ideal state; only through spiritual change, when Hashem is brought into one's sense of reality, is the process able to turn toward perfection. This is why the history of B'nei Yisrael includes the presence of those who served *avodah zarah*. The way that the entire portion of *Maggid* is presented in the Haggadah reflects this idea. The fact that we were slaves isn't merely stated; it serves as an answer to the question of *Mah Nishtanah*—Why is this night different from all of the other nights of the year? It is through the learning process of question and answer that we recognize the need to develop from the sense of *he'edar*, the absence in knowledge, to the higher level of enlightenment. The process that exists within each family unit at the Seder is the same process that the nation as a whole experienced from the time of it being *chosser*. Our forefathers served *avodah zarah*, yet we have developed to the point where we legitimately seek spiritual perfection as being the nation of Hashem.

Therefore, just as the portion of *Maggid* is said in terms of question and answer, so too, the answer had to contain the knowledge that our forefathers had served *avodah zarah*—for such is the developmental process in Hashem's world, from *chessorin* to the lofty state of *sheleimus*.

The *pasuk* toward the end of *Parashas Vayechi* states: "Yosef said to his brothers, 'I will die, but surely G-d will surely remember you and bring you out of this land to the land that He swore to Avraham, Yitzchak, and Yaakov.'"[12] Yosef is revealing to his brothers the process that will occur through which they will eventually be redeemed from their bondage in Mitzrayim. In his transmission to them, he uses the words that represent *geulah*; the double phrase of "*pakod yifkod*." The translation of the double phrase is meant to imply that the redemption will "surely occur." The *Sheim MiShmuel* adds an added dimension to the meaning of this double expression of *geulah*.

Yosef revealed the secret that the person who comes and says these words will be validated as the true *go'el*, redeemer. When Moshe came in *Parashas Shemos* to present himself as the *go'el*, he was not initially accepted. When the *zekeinim*, elders, told Serach bas Asher, the bearer of the secret of the *geulah*, that someone had claimed to be the redeemer, she didn't necessarily consider him valid. But when they informed her that he had said the double *lashon* of *pakod yifkod*, she proclaimed Moshe as the true *go'el*. This *lashon* is not meant to be understood as

12 *Bereishis* 50:24.

some form of secret code transmitted from Yaakov to Yosef and then to the ultimate redeemer, but rather as a phrase that represents the full dimension of the *geulah* of Mitzrayim, which the *go'el*—Moshe—understood was necessary to occur.

The *Sheim MiShmuel* cites the words of the *Ramban* that the word *geulah* reflects a similar concept to *mecher*, a sale.[13] The idea of a sale is not merely that one person relinquishes his ownership on an item, which then becomes *hefker*, ownerless; rather, the ownership of the article leaves one person and is transferred to the person who is purchasing it. This serves as the key to understanding the power of the words *pakod yifkod*.

Chazal reveal that the Torah used four expressions to signify the redemption from Mitzrayim. The *pesukim* at the beginning of *Parashas Va'eira* state:

- "*V'hotzeisi*—I [Hashem] will take you out from under the burdens of Mitzrayim;
- *V'hitzalti*—I will rescue you from their service;
- *V'ga'alti*—I will redeem you with an outstretched arm and with great judgments;
- *V'lakachti*—I will take you to Me for a people."[14]

The first three expressions imply that indeed, B'nei Yisrael will be freed from their terrible bondage in Mitzrayim, but the fourth expression of "*V'lakachti*" reveals that there was a specific purpose that will be a result and outgrowth of their state of freedom: that of serving Hashem and being His nation. Hashem is taking B'nei Yisrael out of Mitzrayim's "ownership" and acquiring them for Himself. It is as if there is a sale occurring, where Mitzrayim is selling the rights to B'nei Yisrael to Hashem and that serves as the completion of the redemption. It is this point that explains the meaning of the double *lashon* of *geulah*.

The true *go'el* will come and reveal that the end goal is not merely freedom; it is the wherewithal to be able to serve Hashem legitimately.

---

13 *Shemos* 6:6.
14 Ibid., 6:6–7.

The *Maharal* in *Nesivos Olam* explains the requirement to directly proceed from the last verse in *Tzur Yisrael*—"Blessed are You Hashem, Who redeemed Yisrael"—to the *Shemoneh Esrei*. The intent of the *Shemoneh Esrei* is our clear proclamation that whatever we have in our lives is a function of Hashem. It is basically a statement that "I need You, [Hashem]." We have no sense of identity without Him, and we therefore totally belong to Him. Yet, if we were actually owned by anyone else, this statement in the *tefillah* would inherently lack legitimacy. Therefore, as an introduction to *tefillah*, we proclaim that we are totally free because Hashem redeemed us from the land of Mitzrayim, and we do not belong to anyone else. Therefore, we can actually be owned by Hashem and serve Him.

When we pray, we are not meant to merely pronounce the words; we are to truly reflect the commitment signified in those words. An *eved Ivri*, a Jewish slave, under certain conditions and guidelines is permitted to marry (without *kiddushin*) a non-Jewish female slave of his master in order to produce additional slaves for him. A regular free *Yid* is not permitted to do this, yet the *eved Ivri* is. The *mefarshim* explain that because the *eved* has acquired his own master, his connection and bond to the ultimate Master, Hashem, becomes somewhat compromised. When we say in the *tefillah* of Pesach that it is "*zeman cheiruseinu*—a time of freedom," it means that because we are free from control and ownership by any human, we are able to dedicate ourselves totally to Hashem. In the *geulah* of Mitzrayim, there is meant to be two parts: one to be free from the bondage of Mitzrayim, and one to be owned by Hashem and be His nation. This paradigm is true in every *galus* we experienced, and in each personal *galus* that any of us go through.

We saw that the *pasuk* in *Parashas Shemos* states: "Go, gather the elders of Yisrael, and say to them: 'Hashem, the G-d of your fathers, the G-d of Avraham, Yitzchak, and Yaakov, appeared to me, saying, "*Pakod pakadati*" (*pakadati* is in the past tense, stating that Hashem has remembered B'nei Yisrael, while *yifkod* is the future tense used by Yosef)—I have indeed been mindful and remembered you, regarding that which is being done to you in Mitzrayim.'"[15] *Rashi* explains that the *zekeinim* would listen to Moshe because this was the sign given over to B'nei Yisrael from Yaakov and Yosef—that with this expression they were to be redeemed. *Pirkei d'Rebbi Eliezer* discusses how the *zekeinim* came before Serach bas Asher and told her of Moshe's words. As we saw, she was not convinced until they informed her that he had used the double expression of *pakod yifkod*; only then did she validate him as the true *go'el*. The *Maharal* in *Gevuros Hashem* explains the words of Chazal regarding the significance of this special phrase.

The words "*pakod yifkod*" and "*pakod pakadati*" signify *geulah* in that there is a doubling of the letter *peh*. The letter *peh* is one of the doubled letters of "*MeNaTzPaCh*," the letters *mem*, *nun*, *tzaddi*, *peh*, and *chaf*. There are twenty-two basic letters of the *aleph-beis*. There are five letters that are unique in that they occur twice, with the second letter being used to close a word. As in the word *mayim*, water, one form of the letter *mem* begins the word while the *mem sofis* ends and completes it. Hashem created the physical and mundane world with the basic twenty-two letters, while creating the "world of *geulah*" with the letters of *MeNaTzPaCh*. The world of *geulah* represents the purpose and *tachlis*, the *gmar* of the world we live in. It is the second dimension of our existence and thus is referenced by the use of the double letters of *MeNaTzPaCh*. Although the letters of *MeNaTzPaCh* that are *sofis* are used to complete the words being expressed, when they are found doubled in a complete phrase—for example, in *pakod yifkod*—this is also a reflection of *geulah*.

Adam HaRishon was created with a *guf*, body, and *neshamah*, soul, and was commanded to elevate his *guf* so that it would be an obedient servant to his *neshamah*. This was to be the role of all physical entities that were created. But Adam sinned, and as a result, the physical framework of the world became dominant, while its spiritual dimension lost its outward prominence. Avraham, Yitzchak, and Yaakov were physical people who walked the earth, but through their exalted spiritual status

15 Ibid., 3:16.

and holy perception, they understood that the purpose of Man's existence lies in the spiritual world of *Olam Haba*. Thus, when the Torah discusses their relationships with their enemies, the people who were totally immersed in a purely physical existence and threatened the ability of the Avos to live in terms of *kedushah*, the Torah uses the double letters of *MeNaTzPaCh*. The first is in terms of this world, while the second is in terms of *geulah* and the world of *kedushah*. The *chaf* is found when Hashem tells Avraham to leave Ur Kasdim and flee from the evil Nimrod, in the *pasuk* of "***Le**ch le**ch**a*."[16] The *mem* is found when Yitzchak is saved from the dominance of the Pelishtim and Avimelech, in the *pasuk* of "*Ki atza**m**ta **mim**enu*."[17] The *nun* is found when Yaakov is saved from his evil brother Eisav, as the *pasuk* says: "*Hatzilei**ni** **Na***."[18] All of these *pesukim* utilize the dual quality of the letters of *MeNaTzPaCh*—although not necessarily in the *sofis* form—in that the letters are doubled. The common denominator of these three expressions is that the Avos were in a state beyond the mundane and physical, the exalted realm created by the letters of *MeNaTzPaCh*. Their salvation occurred because their true connection was to the added realm of *Olam Haba*, and they were therefore granted Hashem's protection in miraculous and metaphysical ways.

This connection is defined as a sense of *geulah*, for it reflects the realization of their spiritual potential, and thus, they were able to live their life in *Olam Hazeh* in its most idealistic form. *Galus* is defined as something that exists within a framework that is not its ideal state, resembling an exiled king who cannot govern as he would under normal conditions. Man is considered in *galus* when he dwells in a world that is truly mundane, where his spiritual potential cannot be realized. Thus, the letters of *MeNaTzPaCh* related to the Avos and their capacity for *geulah*. It is the double letter *peh* that is therefore used to redeem Klal Yisrael from their *shibud*, and this is where the secret of *pakod yifkod* emerges.

---

16 *Bereishis* 12:1.

17 Ibid., 26:16.

18 Ibid., 32:12.

The Avos planted the spiritual seeds through which the nation's identity would be defined by the exalted spiritual realm and not the lowly physical domain. *Yetzias Mitzrayim* was the birth of a nation whose true dimension was beyond the physical realm. The secret represented in *pakod yifkod* is that Moshe didn't merely represent himself as the one who would free B'nei Yisrael from their physical bondage in Mitzrayim, but as the one who would serve as the catalyst to elevate their existence so they could live for *Olam Haba*. The redeemer that would present himself with such a purpose would inherently be virtuous and clearly be the one who bears the truth.

There is an additional point that can serve as a tremendous source of *chizuk* to all of us. The additional letter of the *MeNaTzPaCh* is that of the *tzaddi*. The *tzaddi* will be used to eventually redeem Klal Yisrael from the long and bitter *galus* that we are presently in. The *pasuk* in *Zechariah* says: "Behold, there is a man, ***tz**emach*, *yi**tz**mach*—and he will flourish in his place."[19] This represents the final double phrase referring to when Mashiach will establish Klal Yisrael's existence in the realm of *kedushah*, as befitting the holy children of Avraham, Yitzchak, and Yaakov. From *pakod yifkod* may we soon reap the benefits of *tzemach yitzmach*.

We have seen that *galus* represents the inability to rise to one's spiritual potential, and *geulah* represents the new ability to do so. This explains a somewhat overlooked aspect of the *shirah* at *krias Yam Suf*.

Why did B'nei Yisrael sing?

On a basic level, they had just been saved from annihilation at the hands of the Mitzriyim, and the happiness they felt in their hearts simply overflowed with song. But there is an additional point present that reflects the essence of what *shirah* is. The *mefarshim* discuss two ideas that are represented in the word *shirah*. Although they seem to reflect two opposite interpretations, in truth they reflect the totality of what is represented within the song of *shirah*:

---

19 *Zechariah* 6:12.

- Rav Tzadok explains that the word *shirah* refers to something that resembles a circle composed of various diverse points. He bases this interpretation on the Gemara in *Masechta Bava Metzia*[20] that discusses coins that are found on the ground in the form of a "*shir.*" *Rashi* explains that this is the form of a circle. The *pasuk* in *Parashas Ha'azinu* refers to the entire Torah as a *shirah*, because just as a song is a compilation of the many diverse musical notes that comprise the song, so too, the Torah includes all the elements of existence in Hashem's *briah*. "*Histakel b'Oraisa u'bara alma*—Hashem looked into the Torah and created the world." All events are represented in the Torah, and, in that sense, the Torah includes all. This idea is represented in the circle. The points in a circle seemingly are all joined together to create the totality of the circle.
- The *Sefas Emes* writes that the word *shirah* comes from the word *shur*, a wall that is directly straight from the point of its origin until its end.

These two ideas seem to be opposites. But the *Chiddushei HaRim* unites both ideas with a profound point. The *pasuk* in *Tehillim* states: "Light is sown for the righteous; *u'l'yishrei lev simchah*—and for the upright of heart, gladness."[21] Why does *simchah* result from a sense of *yashrus*, straightness, of the heart? The *Chiddushei HaRim* explains that *yashrus* shows that the person recognizes all the steps that were necessary to reach the goal. The word *shirah* comes from the word *shur*, wall, in that each part of the straight wall is utilized to reach its end. There is no deviation; all that occurred serves the end goal in some way. The end is seen as clearly emanating from its beginning, its source. It is this sense of *yashrus* that results in the profound degree of happiness that elicits *shirah*.

True *shirah* isn't born; it is a function of the sense of chaos of the beginning. The start of *shirah* is the circle where everything seems not in a line or order and everything seems to possess its own agenda. There

---

20 25a.

21 *Tehillim* 97:11.

seems no sense of unification of elements to bring about an ultimate goal. From this state of confusion, he who possesses *yashrus* of the heart is able to perceive that, indeed, there is a method to what is being perceived as sheer madness. Every step is vital to create the ultimate result. When a person is faced with such a sense of truth, supreme *simchah* results. The explosion of that heart in this state of happiness is called *shirah*.

B'nei Yisrael were subject to bitter *shibud* in Mitzrayim. They suffered greatly and yearned for redemption. Ultimately, they were freed and then witnessed and experienced *krias Yam Suf* when the actual Sea of Reeds split and allowed them passage. The secrets of the universe became clear to them at the sea. As a result, they perceived that just as their redemption served to establish their supreme spiritual identity, so too did the *shibud* they had been forced to suffer. The *kur habarzel* that had served to smelt away their impurities had subsequently created their profound spiritual stature. It was bitter, but it was necessary, for all the seemingly diverse elements were required to create the *kedushah* of the *geulah*. Here too, their *shibud* is presented as the *shir*, the circle. But ultimately, the *shibud* led to the perception of their vital role in the cleansing of Klal Yisrael. At that point, it became the *shur*, the straight line that depicted the ingredients of their greatness. It was then that they sang.

"*U'l'yishrei lev simchah*"—when they perceived the straight line directly emanating from the Source, Hashem, unswervingly leading to the fulfillment of the ultimate goal, their hearts exploded in the happiness of *shirah*. True reality cannot be faked, and neither can true happiness. Happiness is *sheleimus*, the completion of all the parts of one's life to be fulfilled through their connection to Hashem. Therefore, they sang *shirah*, for that was what truly depicted the holy process being expressed in their hearts, governed by true *yashrus*—a deep recognition of their newfound ability to know who they always truly were.

Until now, we have been discussing the roots of the bondage of Klal Yisrael resulting from the Avos and our *shibud* in *Mitzrayim*. These represented the *maaseh Avos*; we will now begin to discuss the *siman lebanim*.

Our celebration of Chanukah differs significantly from Purim by its absence of a formal *seudah*, meal. This is because the goal of the Yevanim was not necessarily to kill us, unlike Haman on Purim. This is interesting, because we would have thought that the goal of all our enemies is to destroy us. Indeed, the common thread of true enemies is their desire to destroy their adversaries. Therefore, because Haman and the Yevanim hated us, it would make sense for them to have waged war against us in any way that would allow them to emerge victorious. But the *Maharal* explains in *Ner Mitzvah* (and elsewhere) the profound concept that defines Klal Yisrael's *galus*—exile at the hands of the *Dalet Malchiyos*, the Four Kingdoms—and his discussion deals with this question directly.

The *Maharal* specifically focuses on why there are precisely four kingdoms and not more or less. A person is composed of four basic parts: his *guf*, body; *nefesh*, soul; *seichel*, spiritual intellect; and the *ko'ach*, spiritual force, that coordinates all of the parts as one, the "*me'ached*," from the *lashon* of *echad*, one. The *Maharal* is referring to the different aspects of the soul that are responsible for the *kedushah* that exists in the *guf*, *nefesh*, and *seichel* of each member of Klal Yisrael. Whatever occurs in each person exists in a collective sense within Klal Yisrael as a whole. Therefore, just as the presence of a *cheit* spiritually damages the *kedushah* of a person, a similar process exists within the entire nation. Through *cheit*, Klal Yisrael as an entity becomes spiritually tarnished. As each person is composed of these four elements, the spiritual damage that exists in each of the parts must be cleansed. It is the function of the *Dalet Malchiyos* to attack Klal Yisrael, each in their own way, to enable Klal Yisrael to rise above the challenge and cleanse the *chelek*, part, of the soul being dealt with at that point. The *Maharal* explains the specific onslaught of each of the Kingdoms.

- ***Galus Bavel***: The *chelek* of the soul that the *Maharal* calls *nefesh* is housed in the heart, and in a sense serves as the controller. Basically, it represents the "*etzem*," the basic essence of the person, for it is this *chelek* that is responsible for speech—the definitive quality of a person. The goal of Bavel was to dominate (and thus challenge) the sense of control that is represented in *nefesh*. In the desire of the Babylonians, led by Nebuchadnezzar, to control, they wanted to enslave Klal Yisrael and remove from them their sense of aristocracy and dominion. The goal of their murder of innocent members of Klal Yisrael was a second step; they had their specific agenda and only veered from it in order to ultimately accomplish their basic goal. When Klal Yisrael was redeemed from that exile, they cleansed the collective *chelek* of *nefesh* from its spiritual impurity.

- ***Galus Paras U'Madai***: This was spearheaded by Haman. Their attack was upon the *kedushah* that is inherent in the collective *guf* of Klal Yisrael. Therefore, their focus was to kill the members of the Jewish nation. Regarding the decree of "*L'hashmid l'haarog u'l'abeid*—to destroy, to slay, and to annihilate [the Jews],"[22] the *Gra* asks, What is included in "*u'l'abeid*" that isn't included in "*l'hashmid u'l'haarog*"? He explains that it refers to Haman's desire for the slain members of B'nei Yisrael to not be buried. It represents an attack on the *kedushah* of the "*Yiddishe guf*," which the nations of *Galus Paras U'Madai* sought to destroy and negate. Therefore, the redemption from Haman and Achashveirosh cleansed the impurity of the *chelek* of the soul housed in the *kaved*, liver, that the *Maharal* refers to as "*guf*."
- ***Galus Yavan***: This was different in that the Yevanim related totally to the *chochmah*, wisdom, of the physical world and denied the significance of the true *chochmah* of Torah. Their attack was in terms of the purpose of Man's intellect, his *seichel*. They believed the intellect is meant to exist merely to ponder the mysteries of the physical universe; they resented the idea that it is to be used as a *keli*, vehicle, to enable a human being composed of flesh and blood to relate to Hashem. B'nei Yisrael fought back the onslaught of the Yevanim with *mesiras nefesh*

---

22 *Esther* 3:13.

and thus cleansed the collective *seichel* of Klal Yisrael of any impurity resulting from *cheit*.

- ***Galus Edom***: Interestingly, in this long *galus*, Klal Yisrael has experienced attacks similar to those that were present in the first three exiles. This *galus* corresponds to the *chelek* of *me'ached*; it relates to the other three exiles and is therefore subject to the forms of attack present in them as well. As the first three exiles each correspond to a different aspect of the collective soul of Klal Yisrael, the attacks that occurred in each were tailor-made to the specific *galus*.

The way in which we celebrate our *geulah* from each *galus* corresponds to what was saved. In the *yeshuah*, salvation, of Purim, the *kedushah* of the body was saved, and there is therefore a specific mitzvah to have a *seudah*; in general, the *avodah* of Purim involves physical actions that relate significantly to the *guf*. On Chanukah, there is no specific mitzvah of a *seudah*, but we sing praises to Hashem and light the menorah, producing the *ohr* of the *neiros*, shining to the world. In the attack of the Yevanim, our connection to Torah and spirituality was attacked, and thus on Chanukah we celebrate in ways that relate to the *ohr* of Torah. The goal of the Yevanim wasn't to physically destroy us but rather to spiritually annihilate us. Any killing of B'nei Yisrael was in order for their main objective to be accomplished.

Unfortunately, our enemies do want to destroy us, but each of the exiles have a different form of attack. But Klal Yisrael survives because of the *chessed* of Hashem, as one sheep in the midst of seventy wolves.

Shechinah in Galus

WHEN THE SHEVATIM were talking to their father, Yaakov, the *pasuk* in *Parashas Mikeitz* states: "But if you [Yaakov] will not send him [Binyamin], we will not go down; for the man said to us, 'You will not see my face unless your brother is with you.' Yisrael said, 'Why did you treat me so badly by telling the man that you had another brother?'"[1] *Midrash Rabbah* says that this was the only "*davar shel batalah*—worthless and not proper words" that Yaakov ever said. Hashem was setting the stage that, as viceroy of Mitzrayim, Yaakov's son Yosef would enable B'nei Yisrael to enter their *galus Mitzrayim* in a somewhat easier fashion. Yet Yaakov complains to his sons that their words to the viceroy harmed him and seems to not realize that the entire process was decreed from Hashem.

How can we try to understand the words of Yaakov, the man of *emes*, truth?

The *Maharal* in *Gevuros Hashem* discusses the concept of *galus* and explains that through *galus*, the host nation challenges the exiled people and hopefully causes their spiritual elevation. As with all punishments to Klal Yisrael, *galus* is a vehicle to test and challenge, thus elevating them to greater heights that they wouldn't have attained without it. When challenged, people dig down into their very essence to overcome

1 *Bereishis* 43:5.

any spiritual onslaught that might come their way. However, not just any nation can spiritually challenge another.

The *Maharal* explains in *Ner Mitzvah* that the Four Exiles that we suffered and continue to endure all represent a specific kind of spiritual attack on Klal Yisrael. With regard to the attack of Yavan that resulted in the Yom Tov of Chanukah, the *Maharal* explains that the Yevanim fought against the *seichel*, the holy intellect, of Klal Yisrael. Buried within the collective *seichel* of Klal Yisrael was an element of *ra*, evil, that had to be purged. Only a nation that related to *chochmah* would have the capacity to challenge Klal Yisrael's relationship to their *chochmah—chochmas haTorah*—in order to cleanse them from any impropriety that existed. Thus, it was specifically the Yevanim who, through their strong connection to secular wisdom, could challenge the holy *seichel* of Klal Yisrael.

In other words, in order for one nation to affect Klal Yisrael, there must be a *makom chibbur*, a point of connection, where the challenge can take place. The Greeks' allegiance to *chochmah* was their "*makom chibbur*" with Klal Yisrael.

It is in light of this that Klal Yisrael's initial *galus* in Mitzrayim seems difficult to understand. The land of Mitzrayim is called "*ervas ha'aretz*," representing the most immoral country of the world; they were so steeped in immorality that they actually personified this quality. Klal Yisrael are a moral people. For two hundred and ten years, they were slaves in Mitzrayim, and only one incident of immorality occurred. Even that was nonintentional, occurring with Shlomis bas Divri of *Shevet Dan*. In the *pasuk* in *Parashas Pinchas*, Hashem attached His name "Kah" (composed of *yud* and *heh*) to the names of the *Shevatim* by adding the letter *heh* to the beginning of the name and *yud* to the end of the name (e.g., ***Ha****Reuven****i***, ***Ha****Shimon****i***). This was to bear witness that they were indeed the descendants of the original sons of Yaakov.[2] Where do we see a *makom chibbur* that would enable Mitzrayim to challenge—and thus be the cause to elevate—Klal Yisrael?

---

2 *Bamidbar* 26:7.

The *pasuk* in *Parashas Vayeishev* states: "He [Potiphar] left everything he possessed in the control of Yosef. He did not concern himself with anything about him, except for the bread he ate."[3] *Rashi* teaches us that the *pasuk* of "except for the bread he ate," is euphemistically referring to Potiphar's wife. *Sefarim* explain that the two aspects of the mouth, talking and eating, are linked to the physical desires relating to immorality. Rav Tzadok explains in his *sefer Likutei Maamarim* the connection between the functions of the mouth and the body's capacity for immorality.

In our terms, both the mouth and the *makom bris* of a person share a common goal. A person is composed of a *guf* and *neshamah*. Our relationship with Hashem is based upon our *guf* and *neshamah* existing in a state of *kedushah* fitting to relate to the Creator. The process through which human beings are physically created is necessary for the world to be inhabited in order that there should be people existing to be able to serve Hashem. The inherent *kedushah* in *ishus*, marriage, is based upon this idea, as evidenced in Yaakov's words to his future father-in-law, Lavan.

In *Parashas Vayeitzei* Yaakov says: "Deliver me my wife, for my term is fulfilled, and thus I will consummate the marriage with her."[4] *Rashi* explains that although Yaakov seems to be talking in a fashion that even the "*kal she'b'kalim*," the lowest of the low, would not speak, with regard to Yaakov, his total intent was for the purpose of having children and thereby creating Klal Yisrael. Rav Tzadok explains that "*Yaakov Avinu lo meis*"—his *madreigah* was such that it was as if he didn't die; he was on the spiritual level of Adam HaRishon prior to his *cheit* of eating from the *Eitz Ha'daas*. The consequence of death only emerged after Adam's *cheit*, for prior to that point, he was meant to live and not die. In the world before the *cheit*, there was no evil within Adam, and as such, all his actions were able to flow in absolute *kedushah* and purity without any sense of evil intentions resulting from the internal *yetzer hara* to lead him astray. In line with this, the sole intention of Yaakov's

3 *Bereishis* 39:6.

4 Ibid., 29:21.

words was purely in terms of his *avodas Hashem* to build Klal Yisrael to be Hashem's Nation. Thus, the *kedushah* of the *makom bris* is that it provides the ability for people to serve Hashem.

Similarly, the *peh*, mouth, is the place from where one speaks; through the holy words a person says to another, he is able to spiritually uplift him and bring him closer to Hashem. In a sense, what the *makom bris* does for the *guf*, the *peh* does for the soul. The *pasuk* in *Parashas Lech Lecha* states: "Avram took his wife, Sarai; Lot, his brother's son; and all their possessions that they had amassed; *v'es ha'nefesh asher asu b'Charan*—and the souls they had made in Charan."[5] *Rashi* explains that the souls they made in Charan refer to the people they converted to believe in Hashem. Thus, the words of the *peh* have the ability to "create" as well through bringing people closer to Hashem.

A similar process can be found with regard to eating. One of the ways that Man is able to spiritually elevate his world is through the food that he eats. This occurs because when we eat a food, we say a *berachah*, and thus, this particular food has now been elevated from a mere apple to something being utilized to bring praise to Hashem. The goal of all of the functions of the *peh* and the *makom bris* are meant to be utilized for *kavod Shamayim*, to reveal Hashem's greatness in His world. When not utilized properly, the potential that could have been is wasted. This is the *yesod* for understanding the *makom chibbur* between the immoral land of Mitzrayim and the holy nation of Klal Yisrael.

The *cheit* of Adam HaRishon included the distortions of the spiritual potential of the *peh* and that of the *makom bris*, containing the forbidden fruit and the improper desire of the *nachash* in relation to Chavah. The *berachos* that Yaakov received from Yitzchak in *Parashas Toldos* represented a vital step in the *tikkun* of the *cheit*, which was why they occurred only after the meal prepared by Rivkah. Since the *cheit* included *kilkul*, spiritual damage in terms of eating, the *tikkun* required eating as well.

---

5 Ibid., 12:5.

It is this concept that the *Avnei Nezer* uses to explain *galus Mitzrayim.* In order for B'nei Yisrael to be challenged by Mitzrayim in terms of their stay in *galus*, there had to be a *makom chibbur*. Through the words of Yaakov, there was one. Chazal write of the extraordinary *kedushah* that Yaakov Avinu exhibited, and in that sense, he and his children could not be exiled in Mitzrayim. The distortions of the *makom bris* of Mitzrayim could not challenge the holy B'nei Yisrael. But Yaakov's statement of "why did you do such harm to me?" involved improper speech and therefore created the ability of Mitzrayim, the most immoral land, to become the host for the *galus* of the children of Yaakov. The *kilkul* of Yaakov in terms of the *peh* could be challenged by those who represent *kilkul* in the *makom bris*, for as explained above, they are intrinsically connected.

The *Avnei Nezer* takes this idea a step further to explain a verse in the Haggadah. In the middle of *Maggid* it is written: "He [Yaakov] went down to Mitzrayim, *anus al pi ha'dibbur*—impelled by the speech." This would seem to refer to the speech of Hashem, when He had foretold to Avraham Avinu: "Know for sure that your descendants will be strangers and foreigners in a land that is not theirs, and they will enslave and oppress them for four hundred years." The *Avnei Nezer* writes, however, that it is referring to the speech of Yaakov. He was forced to speak in such a way by Hashem in order for Mitzrayim to be a fitting haven for the *galus* of the children of Yaakov. The destiny of Klal Yisrael was with Mitzrayim, and therefore Yaakov was forced to say something improper to fulfill it, establishing somewhat of a bond with the immorality of Mitzrayim.

The words of Yaakov were improper because ultimately, Hashem was controlling the process of B'nei Yisrael going to Mitzrayim. Similarly, Yosef portrays somewhat of a lack of total trust in Hashem. *Parashas Vayeishev* ends with: "The chief cupbearer did not remember Yosef but forgot him."[6] *Parashas Mikeitz* begins with: "It was at the end of two full years that Pharaoh dreamed."[7] *Rashi* explains that since Yosef depended

6 Ibid., 40:23.

7 Ibid., 41:1.

on the *sar ha'mashkim* to remember him and try to get him out of jail, he remained imprisoned for an additional two years. As the *pasuk* in *Tehillim* says: "Fortunate is the man who has made G-d his trust."[8] The *Beis HaLevi* in his *kuntres* on *Bitachon* quotes a Chazal in *Midrash Rabbah* that the proper way to view the ultimate release of Yosef from prison was not because Pharaoh dreamed but because Hashem decreed that Yosef should be freed. To facilitate the Will of Hashem, Pharaoh subsequently dreamed. The *pasuk* in *Iyov* states: "He [Hashem] sets a limit to the darkness."[9] Yosef remained in jail for that was the decree of Hashem. When the decree changed, then and only then, did Pharaoh actually dream.

Both Yaakov and Yosef, on their exalted spiritual levels, failed to an extent to recognize that what was occurring was all part of Hashem's master plan. But when the meeting between Yaakov and his long-lost precious son occurred, Yosef revealed the inner meaning of what had transpired, and Yaakov was finally at peace.

There is a basic question relating to when Yaakov and Yosef were finally reunited. What was so special about the wagons Yosef sent his father that after Yaakov saw them, he was relieved? This question is based upon the *pasuk* in *Parashas Vayigash*: "He saw the wagons that Yosef had sent to transport him, then the spirit of their father was revived."[10] All the years Yaakov had been inconsolable over the loss of Yosef, yet when he saw the wagons, it triggered in him a sense of spiritual revival. The Berditchiver, in his *sefer Kedushas Levi*, reveals the key to Yaakov's renewal.

The *tachlis* of all existence is for Man to recognize Hashem as the *Shoresh*, Root, of everything; a world where this can't result would defy the inner meaning of the universe. Yaakov was inconsolable, for in his loss of Yosef, he thought that the spiritual *tachlis* of Yosef would never be realized. Yosef's role was to take the essence of the exalted Avos and enable it to be transmitted to the future of Klal Yisrael. To that end,

---

8 *Tehillim* 84:6.
9 *Iyov* 28:3.
10 *Bereishis* 27:45.

his brothers had to bow down to him, as revealed in Yosef's dreams, to acknowledge their need to accept his sovereignty and what he had to offer. Without that capacity, Yaakov feared all would be lost.

It is difficult to understand on what level Yosef would be able to reveal to Yaakov the true meaning of suffering, but the Berditchiver explains that Yosef's sending of the wagons represented his personal plight and the meaning of all the trials and tribulations that he had been destined to endure. The Torah focuses on the fact that the wagons were specifically sent from Yosef and thus implied some sense of message. The *pasuk* says: "And he saw the wagons that Yosef had sent," and Yaakov understood the message Yosef was revealing to him. The word in *lashon hakodesh* for wagons is *agalos*, from the word *igul*, circle, because the way a wagon moves is through the rolling of the wheel.

A wheel rolls to create movement, and through this Yosef revealed the meaning of tragedy to Yaakov. The process of movement in a wheel occurs when the first step, the beginning of the movement, leads to the next step, its further movement based upon the continued roll of the wheel. *Ra*, evil, as the *Maharal* writes many times, is not a *metzius*, a true identity in its own right, but only exists to in some way reveal the true *metzias*: *tov*, good.

There seems to be no doubt that Yosef being sold to Mitzrayim, and the many trials he was subjected to, is to be considered a function of *ra* and a most profound *cheit* on the part of the *Shevatim*. Yet, Yosef told his brothers, although they sold him to Mitzrayim as an act of evil, Hashem had other plans: Yosef was sent to Mitzrayim before B'nei Yisrael to pave the way for a nation to be able to exist in the *ervas ha'aretz*, the most immoral place, and yet be able to retain their own sense of *kedushah* and *yichus* from one generation to another. His role was to give life—the physical life he provided through his distribution of the grain he had stored, as well as the spiritual life he supplied to the internal soul of Klal Yisrael. When "*va'yanus ha'chutzah*,"[11] when Yosef ran away and overcame the challenge of the wife of Potiphar, he instilled in B'nei

---

11 Ibid., 39:13.

Yisrael their eternal capacity to remain holy. Every step in his personal tragedy and the trials that occurred were all to create the ultimate *tov* that was meant to develop out of them. Thus, the *ra* in itself had no productive purpose, but within the context of Hashem's ultimate Will, it was necessary to lead to the goal of the revelation of the *tov*. As the wheel rolls on and the first step of the wheel leads to the furthering of the movement, Yosef was revealing to Yaakov that the plight he had suffered was to lead him to the state where he could ultimately emerge spiritually upright and victorious. At first, Yaakov didn't believe the brothers when they told him that Yosef was alive and the ruler over all of Mitzrayim. The *pasuk* uses the words of "*va'yafag libo*—his heart rejected it,"[12] and thus he couldn't believe them. The pain and suffering he had experienced deep within his heart could not be comforted. But when he saw the wagons that Yosef had sent, his spirit was revived. It didn't dry the tears of mourning he had shed during those long twenty-two years, but he saw the wagons and thereby understood the meaning of his suffering. He understood what had been required for Yosef to become the *mashbir* over all the land of Mitzrayim.

Our ability to acquire a sense of peace with regard to our lives lies with our total appreciation of this Chazal. Every *sar ha'mashkim* that we meet and wish to rely on will unfortunately forget us, as occurred with Yosef. But in the end, Yosef understood and revealed this to Yaakov and B'nei Yisrael. "He [Hashem] sets a limit to the darkness," and with Him can be found the ultimate control of our destiny. May we be *zocheh* to the words of *Aleinu* that proclaim: "You are to know this day and *take to your heart* that Hashem is the only G-d in heaven above and on the earth below."

Interestingly, Chazal say that to a degree, *dibbur*, speech, was in *galus*, too, while B'nei Yisrael were locked within their *shibud Mitzrayim*. Obviously, this is a very deep concept, but we will attempt to understand it.

---

12 Ibid., 45:26.

In *lashon hakodesh*, Biblical Hebrew—literally, the "holy tongue"—an object or thing is referred to as a "*davar*." *Lashon hakodesh* is referred to as holy because the words that compose it are not arbitrary words that happen to be mere labels for things; they are words that reflect the essence of existence for the items they represent. The word *davar* is no different in that it truly reflects the essence of what it represents. A thing is called *davar*, for everything is a function and result of the *d'var Hashem*—the Word of Hashem that created it. It is this life-providing force emanating from Hashem that becomes the *davar*—the thing itself.

The Mishnah in *Pirkei Avos* that begins the fifth *perek* states: "*B'asarah maamoros*...—With ten utterances the world was created." Hashem said there should be light, and as a result of His word, the element of light came into existence. This is why a thing is called a *davar*; its existence is based on the *d'var Hashem* that created it. It is within this context that one aspect of *dibbur*—being in *galus*—can be understood.

The *Ramban* asks a question on the wording of the first of the *Aseres HaDibros*, Ten Commandments, that were given on Har Sinai. The *pasuk* in *Parashas Yisro* says: "I am Hashem, your G-d, Who has taken you out of the land of Mitzrayim from the house of slavery."[13] Theoretically, there was something even greater than Hashem having taken us out of Mitzrayim: the fact that He created the universe. This would seem to warrant our allegiance and service to Him as servants more so than the *geulah* from Mitzrayim. Thus, the *Ramban* asks, why wasn't that feat mentioned in the *Aseres HaDibros* rather than *yetzias Mitzrayim*. The *Sefas Emes* answers that through the miracles and wonders of *yetzias Mitzrayim*, we were able to appreciate that Hashem had created the world and that He is the One still running it.

During the time that Mitzrayim was being punished with the ten *Makkos*, Hashem was manipulating *teva* at His Will. The Creator had said that there should be light; by causing darkness during the ninth *Makkah*, He revealed Himself as the Creator. Thus, when Hashem said that He took B'nei Yisrael out of Mitzrayim, this represents that He

13 *Shemos* 20:2.

indeed created the world. It was through the process of *yetzias Mitzrayim* that the *d'var Hashem* that had created everything could be recognized as the true Source for all that exists. During the time prior to *yetzias Mitzrayim*, one could not perceive that everything comes from Hashem, so it was as if His *dibbur* was in *galus*. But through *yetzias Mitzrayim*, the word of Hashem was "redeemed," for B'nei Yisrael then understood that He was the Source of everything that exists.

A dimension of the idea of *dibbur* in *galus* can also be related to B'nei Yisrael. Hashem created Man with a sense of a dual identity. His body was formed from the dirt of the ground while his soul is a *chelek Elokei mi'maal*, part of Hashem from Above. This combination provides him with his ability to speak. Man's speech represents his soul being projected into a physical world through his physical body. Hashem established mankind with such a spiritual capacity in order that it should be used to serve Hashem through his words of Torah and *tefillah*. But during their *shibud Mitzrayim*, they were *batul*, negated, to their hosts and lacked their own sense of identity. Their *ko'ach ha'dibbur*, power of speech, was not able to accomplish its intended purpose as a tool to serve the Creator. Pharaoh himself had sinned against Hashem through his own speech when he said to Moshe, "Who is Hashem that I should listen to His voice to send out Yisrael? I do not know Hashem, nor will I send out Yisrael!"[14] With the *geulah* and creation of Klal Yisrael, the *ko'ach ha'dibbur* of Man was able to reach its goal when B'nei Yisrael sang the *shirah* of *Az Yashir*, recognizing Hashem as their G-d and that they will glorify Him. Thus, although both dimensions of *dibbur* were in *galus*, through the *avodah* of B'nei Yisrael, Hashem's role as the Creator, as well as Klal Yisrael's ability to use their speech to serve Him, were accomplished and revealed.

We have seen that the *devar Hashem* is really only fully perceived with the *geulah*. Does that indicate that Hashem Himself is inaccessible during *galus*?

---

14 Ibid., 5:2.

In order to begin to answer this question, let us consider Rachel Imeinu. She was the preferred wife of Yaakov Avinu, so why was she buried on the road and not in the Cave of Machpeilah in Chevron?

The *Maharal* states many times that "*devarim gedolim einam b'mikrah*—Great things are not merely coincidence." That Rachel was buried *b'derech*, on the road, is indeed a *davar gadol*. The *Maharal* in *Netzach Yisrael* discusses this most profound point.

Bereishis Rabbah cites the following *pasuk*: "A voice is heard on high, wailing, bitter weeping, Rachel weeps for her children; she refuses to be consoled for her children, for they are gone. Thus, said Hashem: 'Restrain your voice from weeping and your eyes from tears; for there is reward for your accomplishment,' the word of Hashem, 'And they will return from the enemy's land.'"[15] Rachel Imeinu's role is to plead for *rachamim*, mercy. The *Maharal* explains that it is specifically Rachel who pleads because she represents the *bayis*, the sense of the "home" of Yaakov Avinu. The *ishah*, wife, of a person represents the one who is *me'ached*, coordinates and unites all the parts of the *bayis* to function in an ideal state. Through the *ishah*, all members of the household are able to function in the way in which they were destined.

Rachel is the *akeres ha'bayis*, the mainstay of Yaakov's house. All the years that Yaakov worked for Lavan was for the purpose of marrying Rachel. The Gemara in *Masechta Gittin*[16] quotes Rabbi Yossi, who said that he never referred to his wife as *ishti* but rather as "*baisi*—my home." Thus, Rachel served the role as the *bayis* and as the coordinator of all that is represented in the holy *bayis* of Yaakov. All Klal Yisrael is referred to in terms of Rachel, her children, and grandchildren, as mentioned in the *pasuk*: "*Ha'ben yakir li Ephraim*—Is Ephraim My favorite son?"[17] It was because she was the mainstay of Yaakov's house and represented the entire nation of Klal Yisrael that she was specifically buried *b'derech*.

---

15 *Bereishis Rabbah* 82:10.

16 52a.

17 *Yirmiyahu* 31:19.

Klal Yisrael was sent into *galus*, and it looked as if their greatness was merely something of the past. Yet their greatness was to be considered dormant and not, *chalilah*, dead. It took spiritual strength to keep that capacity alive. The address of the person who served the role as the *me'ached*, coordinator, was Rachel. She had to be buried *b'derech*, on the road—and away from her "home" buried together with Yaakov—in order to be together with her children. They were her children, for she was the *akeres ha'bayis* of Yaakov's home, and thus she was able to keep Klal Yisrael unified even in *galus*. Had she been buried hidden in the cave together with Yaakov, her capacity to relate to her children would have been compromised.

There is an additional idea that relates to Rachel having been buried *b'derech* and crying for her children.

The *pasuk* says: "Thus said Hashem; 'Restrain your voice from weeping and your eyes from tears; for there is reward for your accomplishment.'" Rachel cried tears because of the tragedies that befell her children. But ultimately, it was our tears that the Bnei Yisrael shed as a result of the evil report of the *meraglim* who went to seek out the land of Canaan that were the cause of those tragedies. They cried for nothing, and their punishment was that they would indeed have a legitimate reason for crying when they would be exiled with the destruction of the Beis Hamikdash. It is as if Rachel's tears served as a form of *kapparah* for her children, to enable them to once again return to their land and their former, lofty spiritual stature. When one cries, the reality that's before him becomes blurred. The word in *lashon hakodesh* for tears is *dema'os*, from the word *dimua*, meaning a mixture. For indeed, when one cries, all reality becomes a blurred mixture and is thereby negated. In a sense, it enables one to begin anew with a new set of rules. It is Rachel's tears that are always with us in our long and tragic *galus* all through the years. She is the *akeres ha'bayis* of Yaakov, and she is the one who is *me'ached* her beloved children wherever they are. Thus, her tears lead to our ultimate salvation when we will once again return to our land.

We have seen that Rachel Imeinu was, so to speak, with us in *galus*. As we will see, her presence was representative of Hashem's Presence, as well.

The Gemara in *Masechta Shabbos*[18] discusses the mitzvah of lighting the *Menorah* in the Beis Hamikdash. The Gemara asks: "Does He [Hashem] need the light of the *Menorah*?" The Gemara continues to say that for the forty years that Klal Yisrael traveled in the *midbar*, they were given light by Hashem through the *ananei ha'kavod*, the Clouds of Glory, and the *amud aish*, the pillar of fire. It is therefore clear that the purpose of the *Menorah* is not as a provider of physical light; it is rather to reflect a sense of *kedushah*—that the Shechinah dwells in Klal Yisrael. The exact same amount of oil was placed in each cup, including the *ner maaravi*, yet miraculously—even though it was lit first—it burned the longest. The Gemara says that this serves to portray the presence of the Shechinah in us. Rav Tzadok, in *Resisei Laylah*, discusses a different point that might enable us to appreciate what the Gemara in Shabbos is revealing to us.

The *pasuk* that begins the fifth *perek* of *Megillas Esther* states: "Now it came to pass on the third day, *va'tilbash Esther malchus*—and Esther donned royalty and stood in the inner court of the King's palace." The basic understanding of the words, "*Va'tilbash Esther malchus,*" refers to the royal garments that Esther cloaked herself with when she came before Achashveirosh to plead for the salvation of her people. *Rashi* cites Chazal, who reveal to us that the *malchus*, royalty, that she donned not only refers to physical garments, but to the spiritual dimension of *ruach ha'kodesh*, Divine inspiration, that she enveloped herself within. Rav Tzadok explains the profound point that Chazal are revealing.

One would assume that at the moment when Esther stood before Achashveirosh, the *ruach ha'kodesh* she was privy to was a form of external prophecy or vision that Hashem bestowed upon her. Rav Tzadok explains that this was not the case; she related to the sense of *malchus* that is present in the *lev* of a *Yid*. The *neshamah* of every member of Klal Yisrael is a *chelek Elokei mi'maal*. It is a spiritual element that

18 22b.

constantly exists as the holy spiritual *neshamah* that we were *zocheh* to receive. Thus, it wasn't that Esther received a sense of external vision, but rather, she was able to totally relate and connect to the Presence of Hashem that *already* existed in her heart. As a result, she was able to proceed accordingly and glean the result she desired from her evil husband, Achashveirosh. This is something we all have the capacity to do, but we would have to be spiritually prepared and in tune with the lofty spiritual dimension that dwells within us.

The *Sefas Emes* explains a similar idea in terms of the Shechinah, portrayed through the *ner maaravi*. The *ner maaravi* is a pure *neis*—and miracles give us a peek of the One Who is truly running the world. It is not just that Hashem performs a miracle through the *ner maaravi*; it is that He commanded a human being, the Kohen, to light the *ner* that will burn within the framework of a *neis*. Where do we as humans acquire the capacity for our physical actions to be able to directly develop into a *neis*? It is this point that the Gemara in *Masechta Shabbos* is teaching us. The fact that it is the Kohen who lights the miraculous *ner maaravi* shows clearly that Hashem's Shechinah dwells in Klal Yisrael—in each one of us. Just like with Esther, it wasn't something that existed as an external *neis*, it was a function of the Presence of Hashem that actually resides within us. Our *neshamah* is a *chelek* of Hashem and our actions are a function of its existence. Therefore, the *Menorah*—and the *ner maaravi*—was indeed not for light, but rather to portray that Hashem dwells inside of us as our souls. This is how we survived *galus* in the past, it is how we survive *galus* today, and it is what the candles of Chanukah that commemorate the kindling of the menorah of the Beis Hamikdash teach us in the middle of the trials of our lives. Hashem is with us in the darkness.

The *pasuk* in the beginning of *Parashas Vayechi* states: "Yaakov lived in the land of Mitzrayim seventeen years. The days of Yaakov, the years of his life were one hundred and forty-seven years."[19] The opening *Rashi*

---

19 *Bereishis* 47:28.

in this *parashah* discusses the reason why the *parashah* is referred to as *stumah*, closed. Normally, there exists a space in the Torah between one *parashah* and the *parashah* that follows it. But between *Parashas Vayigash* and *Vayechi* there is no separation. *Rashi* reveals to us two ideas:

- The *shibud Mitzrayim* was now beginning, and the hearts and eyes of B'nei Yisrael were closed because of their bondage.
- The sense of closing refers to what happened to Yaakov himself. Upon gathering all his children together, Yaakov desired to reveal the *keitz*, End of Days, but it became closed and concealed from him.

There seem to be two distinct interpretations being presented in the words of *Rashi*. The *Sefas Emes* reveals to us that indeed, both ideas reflect a common theme.

The *parashah* begins with the word *vayechi*, which means that "he lived." The *Sefas Emes* explains that the Torah chose this word as opposed to the word of *vayehi*, which simply means that "he was." The implication is that although Yaakov was seemingly locked within the *tumah* of the land of Mitzrayim, he was able to *live* a true life and soar beyond those worldly constraints and attach himself to the *Mekor*, the true Source, Hashem, even while living in that lowly land. The *Maharal* reveals to us that the last years of Yaakov's life while in Mitzrayim represented the ultimate *sof*, endpoint, of Klal Yisrael—their destiny to exist in the World to Come and relate totally to Hashem. Yaakov understood clearly and absolutely that anything that seems to contradict the Presence of Hashem is purely in a state of *hester*, where the truth is being hidden within the *metzarim*, confines, of the attachment to the physical world that defined the land of Mitzrayim. *Resha'im*, evil people, are considered as dead, because they are absorbed within the confines of the materialistic world and have thus severed their connection to Hashem, the Source of life. It was this idea that Yaakov had wished to reveal to his children.

Yaakov wanted the *Shevatim* to understand the ultimate destiny of Klal Yisrael—the secret that no matter where one is placed, the connection to Hashem can be alive and vibrant—and to reveal when the time of the *keitz* would occur. Hashem chose to hide those secrets from him, and Yaakov began saying other words. Yaakov meant to reveal to them that the key to all understanding is the total connection to Hashem. Within that framework, there is no *galus*, for one is constantly connected to the Source. The secret of when Klal Yisrael will be redeemed was beyond his ability to reveal, but he was able to tell them that they possessed the capacity to recognize the truth even though they were in the midst of the *hester* of *shibud Mitzrayim*. It was within this framework that *Rashi*'s two ideas merge.

Yaakov wasn't permitted to reveal to his children the *keitz* openly but had to discuss other revelations instead. Connecting with Hashem within the *hester* was the content of his words to them, which represented the *devarim acheirim* of Yaakov. As a result, the *shibud Mitzrayim* began. Had Yaakov revealed the *keitz* openly, and how all is a function of Hashem, there would have been no sense of *hester* and thus no *shibud*. But the *shibud* had to begin, for this was decreed to Avraham Avinu during his *nevuah* of the *Bris Bein Ha'besarim*. This explains why Yaakov's vision of the *keitz*, as well as the eyes and heart of B'nei Yisrael being "closed" as a result of the *shibud*, were actually two sides of the same coin.

Both the words in *lashon hakodesh* for exile, *galus*, and redemption, *geulah*, are spelled with the *shoresh* of a *gimmel* and *lamed*, which spells *gal*, meaning "to reveal." They share this root because Klal Yisrael's exiles are merely instances where the Presence of Hashem isn't openly revealed, but it exists nonetheless. When one perceives the Presence of Hashem within the *galus* itself, one has the capacity to live a life where all *shibud* ceases to truly exist. Yaakov Avinu was able to live in that realm in the last years of his life that were spent in Mitzrayim. For in the words that Yaakov did speak to his children, the true meaning of *galus* was actually revealed, forever.

Beis Hamikdash

THE DESTRUCTION OF the Beis Hamikdash represents the collective sense of the tragedies that occurred to Klal Yisrael on their march to *Acharis HaYamim*. When there was a question regarding the establishment of a specific day to mourn the destruction that occurred during the Second World War, the *Gedolei Yisrael* decided there was no day more fitting than Tishah B'Av. For on that day, Klal Yisrael succumbed to their enemies, and this therefore reflects the day Hashem's nation is steeped in *aveilus*. When B'nei Yisrael cried their "*bechiah shel chinam*—tears of naught" due to the *lashon hara* of the *meraglim* on the ninth of Av, Hashem decreed that on that day, they will indeed have something of substance over which to shed tears.

Perhaps by understanding what the Beis Hamikdash really was, it will help us to understand what we lost. The Torah, in *Parashas Toldos*, tells us that Yitzchak dug wells. These were the wells that his father Avraham had originally dug, which were closed up by the Pelishtim. The Torah tells us that the first two wells Yitzchak dug were once again closed by the Pelishtim, but the third survived and remained opened. The *Ramban* questions why the Torah felt these events had to be known. What glory is being bestowed upon Yitzchak in his "mundane" problems with the Pelishtim, who seemingly emerged successful over him? Why does the Torah need to reveal this in such detail? The *Ramban* answers that this episode represents a profound *sod* with regard to the future of Klal Yisrael.

The *Ramban* teaches us that these wells represent more than just deep pools of water; they reflect the three Batei Mikdash that would later be built:

- The first two wells were closed by the Pelishtim, and these refer to the First and Second Batei Mikdash that were ultimately destroyed.
- Regarding the third well, the Torah says: "*V'lo ravu aleha*—The Pelishtim did not quarrel over it."[1] It was left to remain as a functioning well. This refers to the Third Beis Hamikdash that will be built and will never be destroyed.

The future *churbanos* of Klal Yisrael were being revealed through what occurred with Yitzchak, and it was for this reason that it was written. The profound point the Torah reveals through the wells serves to give us a glimpse of what the Beis Hamikdash actually represented.

The Torah in *Parashas Shemos* teaches us that when Moshe wished to marry, he went to a *be'er*, well. There he met Tzipporah, whom he ultimately married. The *Maharal* in *Gevuros Hashem* explains that Moshe went to a well because Yaakov had gone to a well to meet his wife. Eliezer, the servant of Avraham, had also gone to a well to find a wife for his master Yitzchak.

The *Maharal* explains why a well is suited for such a purpose. Heaven is understood as being the source for all that is utilized upon earth. Everything is bestowed from above down to earth in order to be utilized by Man. Rainwater falls from the sky above and is thereby able to provide life for the world below. It falls naturally and is immediately for use by those on earth. This is where the water of a well differs qualitatively from rainwater. The water of an underground well lacks the natural ability to be elevated and usable. Man himself must first elevate the water that dwells below, and only through his actions can its potential be realized. In a sense, it is a system of growth, where we can hoist the imperfect and unfulfilled to the lofty plane of meaningful existence and purpose. It was for this reason that our great ancestors went to wells.

---

1 *Bereishis* 26:22.

The state of marriage is one of perpetual growth, where imperfection is elevated by hard work to create a complete and fulfilled unit. It is at the well where Man should seek a wife, for it is here that represents the state of marriage. The *Shem MiShmuel* uses this concept to explain the words of the *Ramban*.

The Gemara says that the *makom Aron*, the exact place where the Ark in the Holy of Holies rested, was "*eino min ha'middah*"[2]—it took up no physical space. Incredibly, its actual size didn't diminish the physical capacity of the area in which it was housed.

The Beis Hamikdash is to be considered the embassy of Hashem on earth. An embassy represents a place that, while physically composed of elements of the host nation, has been transformed to be a piece of the nation it serves to represent. Hashem, Who "resides" in heaven, also established His embassy on earth, and that is the Beis Hamikdash. It is here where He dwells, and therefore the place of connection, the *makom Aron*, defies natural physical law. Just as in heaven there are no physical rules and restrictions, so too in His embassy on earth, the *Aron* consumes no physical space. The word *aron* comes from the word *ohr*, light; it's true existence is spiritual. The boxes of gold and wood shed their physical restraints and became part of heaven, and this represents the ultimate *be'er*. The Beis Hamikdash is the supreme place where something on a lower level can be raised to the ultimate spiritual domain and relinquish its *gashmiyus*, its physical dimension. The Torah chose the well to serve as a representative of the Beis Hamikdash because ultimately, the Beis Hamikdash is the definitive *be'er* that exists in our physical world.

Hashem created us with a *guf* composed of the elements of this world, and He established our domain as the ground upon which we tread. Yet, we are commanded to develop our spiritual sense of identity through our *neshamah*, the holy soul we possess that is a part of Hashem. How is that to be accomplished? The answer lies in the holy building that stood in Yerushalayim, the center of the universe. Through its wood and gold, together with the *avodah* that transpired within its walls, the capacity

---

2 *Masechta Bava Basra* 99a.

to grow was transmitted to the hearts of Klal Yisrael. Chazal reveal to us that our enemies, "*kimcha techina techinas*—ground flour that was already ground."[3] The Babylonians and Romans were only able to burn the physical structure of Hashem's House because we, through our actions, had destroyed its heart and soul. The sense of growth that was symbolized by the physical Beis Hamikdash was to serve as a vehicle for *bilvavi Mishkan evneh*—to create a Beis Hamikdash in the heart of stone which is Man; to enable one's *lev* to grow into a spiritual heart, albeit composed of flesh, enabled to properly relate to his Creator. When we destroyed our ability to do that, the *keli* that was to enable our holiness could be destroyed. The Beis Hamikdash as a symbol of ultimate growth was meant to foster our potential to grow; its destruction was therefore a function of our spiritual decay.

The type of *churban* we experienced during *galus Yavan* was markedly different than the physical damage of "*kimcha techina techinas*." The Babylonians and Romans "ground up" the Beis Hamikdash, while the Yevanim allowed it to continue to stand. They had no objection to the existence of a beautiful and majestic building; their war was solely based on the destruction of any *kedushah* deemed to be present. They didn't physically destroy the *shemen*, oil; they spiritually defiled it by making it *tamei*. They represented a people who were totally dedicated to the external and denied the presence of any internal spiritual mechanism within Man.

However, as occurred with Yitzchak and the third well, we look forward to the time when the Third Beis Hamikdash will be rebuilt, and we will once again be able to experience the growth that is the essence of our spiritual life. This idea may help us to relate to the tragic loss our nation endured so many years ago.

The Gemara in *Masechta Gittin*[4] relates the episode of a certain man who had a friend named Kamtza and an enemy named Bar Kamtza. The

3 *Eichah Rabasi* 1:43; *Sanedrin* 96b.

4 55b.

person made a banquet and instructed his attendant to invite Kamtza. The attendant made a mistake and invited Bar Kamtza, who came to the banquet instead. When the host realized the mistake, he told Bar Kamtza, his enemy, to leave. Bar Kamtza did not want the embarrassment of having to leave and offered to pay for the banquet if he could only stay, but to no avail. Seeing that the *Rabbanim* had watched but said nothing when he was being shamed, Bar Kamtza devised a plan that ultimately led to the destruction of Yerushalayim.

Kamtza is seemingly absent from this story as he himself did not come to the party, while only Bar Kamtza plays a role in that he was hated by the host. The Gemara, however, says that the responsibility lies with both of them. The question is, why? The *Maharal* in *Netzach Yisrael* discusses this point and adds an amazing insight.

The word *kamtza* is not just a name. It means "separate" and "isolated." The species of *arbeh*, locusts, are referred to as "*kamtza*." The *pasuk* in *Mishlei* says: "There is no king to the locust."[5] The species of *arbeh* exists in tremendous numbers and is therefore given its name from the word *ribui*, great multitudes. They are called *kamtza* because they lack any coordination or unified posture.[6] The role of a king is to serve his subjects and to provide them with a cohesive identity. The sense of *ribui* that exists with regard to locusts defies the presence of a king, and the multitudes therefore lack the capacity to be united in any way.

The Gemara in *Masechta Berachos* discusses the meaning of people's names and how they define the essence of a person. Thus, the name Bar Kamtza depicts a person who personifies isolation and divisiveness, similar to the status of *arbeh*. He thus played a vital role in the destruction of the Second Beis Hamikdash.

The First Beis Hamikdash was destroyed because of the three cardinal sins of idol worship, immorality, and murder. The First Beis Hamikdash portrayed awesome *kedushah*, a profound Divine Presence. Thus, what succeeded in causing its destruction were acts that defied—and in a sense, contaminated—its purity and holiness.

---

5 *Mishlei* 30:27.

6 Mishnah, *Eduyos* 8:4.

The Second Beis Hamikdash, although holy, lacked the *Aron* and was not at the level of the First Beis Hamikdash. Rather, the *Maharal* explains, it stood as a unifying element within the nation. There was one Kohen Gadol, one *Mizbei'ach*, and one place of *avodah*. This is why what destroyed it was *sinas chinam*, the hatred of one Jew to another, as it was this that shattered the sense of unity. Bar Kamtza was identified with this quality and therefore played a role in the destruction of the Second Beis Hamikdash.

The *Maharal* goes on to explain the role of Kamtza. There are many reasons for the relationships people have with one another. One would think that harmony and friendship are based upon affection, while animosity is based upon hatred. But such is not always the case. Kamtza's name implies divisiveness, and this indicates that his friendship with the host wasn't one of intrinsic affection, but rather a sense of connection to be utilized for the ultimate purpose of separating people. This resembles what sometimes occurs when two warring nations temporarily forget their true feelings in order to bond and fight a mutually hated third country. Kamtza didn't stand for hatred to the same extent as Bar Kamtza, whose name depicted one with a firm connection to hatred. For example, when a thirteen-year old comes of age, he is fully obligated to serve Hashem and is therefore referred to as a "bar mitzvah." The word *bar* means the "son of," and so "bar mitzvah" means he is now totally defined by that stature. Similarly, Bar Kamtza was totally defined by *sinas chinam*, while Kamtza was, too, but to a lesser degree. It was this quality that proved devastating and caused the *churban*.

As mentioned earlier, the specific spiritual characteristics of the Second Beis Hamikdash differed drastically to that of the First. The Gemara in *Masechta Bava Basra* teaches us that King Hurdus extinguished the light of the world by annihilating the *Rabbanim*.[7] He chose to rebuild the Beis Hamikdash in an attempt to gain forgiveness and thereby replace the spiritual light of the world. The Gemara says that whoever did not see the building of Hurdus did not see a truly beautiful

7 4a.

building in all his days. He built the walls with stones of green and white marble. He had wanted to overlay these with gold covering but was told to leave the marble exposed so that from afar, it would appear as the *galei ha'yam*, the waves of the sea. Rav Yitzchok Hutner once explained what was so special about the waves.

The First Beis Hamikdash had the ability to exist *l'netzach* and not be destroyed. The *Maharal* in *Netzach Yisrael* explains that the Second Beis Hamikdash lacked the supreme *kedushah* that was present in the First Beis Hamikdash and was destined to suffer destruction. When a person senses that his *avodah* will be in any way temporary, his spiritual zest and dedication wanes. To protect against that possibility, the walls of the Second Beis Hamikdash were not covered with gold, but instead appeared as the *galei ha'yam*. The waves of the sea are unique because although when they come close to the seashore they dissipate, until that last moment they storm with all their power and prowess. The lead wave dissolves, but then another storms in behind it only to be dissolved as well. This process continues, reflecting the quality of the waves. In their time, they storm, even though they know that they will eventually disintegrate. So too, B'nei Yisrael were to understand the dedication that was needed during the Second Beis Hamikdash. Even though it would eventually be destroyed, in its time, one had to perform his *avodah* with complete dedication. It stood to create *achdus* in Klal Yisrael, and this is why it was *sinas chinam* that destroyed it.

Kamtza's affectionate relationship with the host was a tool both used to foster hate and *machlokes*, strife, with others. Hatred was being perpetuated by the people of the day, and the name Kamtza was a reflection of all his relationships, which were founded upon the spread of *sinas chinam* and ultimately led to the destruction of the Second Beis Hamikdash. Therefore, while Bar Kamtza was the key player within the tale of the actual tragedy of the *churban*, Kamtza also added his specific brand of fuel to the collective fire of *sinas chinam* that was rampant during the time of the Second Beis Hamikdash.

And Chazal reveal to us that, ultimately, it was the specific dimensions of hatred that existed in terms of all the players of that banquet that led to the destruction of Yerushalayim and of the Beis Hamikdash.

Chanukah is all about the rededication of the Beis Hamikdash. Unfortunately, even after the victory of the Chashmona'im, the Second Beis Hamikdash did not last.

The *pasuk* in *Yirmiyahu* states: "And if you do not heed this, My soul will cry in its hidden chambers because of your haughtiness; and if tears will flow, My eye will drop tears, for the flock of Hashem will have been captured."[8] While we understand that the destruction of the Beis Hamikdash was a tragedy, what does it mean that Hashem cries because of it?

The Gemara in *Masechta Chagigah*[9] explains that the three mentions of tears in the *pasuk* represent three dimensions of crying. Two are due to the destruction of the First and Second Batei Mikdash, and the third is for B'nei Yisrael, who were banished from their land. Yet Hashem is above and beyond human frailty, so how are we to understand the notion that He cries? The *Maharal* in *Netzach Yisrael* discusses this point and reveals to us a vital *yesod*.

Whenever anything is mentioned in terms of our perception of Hashem, it is never to be understood as about Hashem Himself. The *Maharal* explains that it is to be understood according to the capacity of the *mekabel*, the receiver. Therefore, when Hashem slew the Mitzriyim at *krias Yam Suf*, He was perceived as a warrior, and when He gave and taught the Torah to Moshe and Klal Yisrael at Har Sinai, He was perceived as a *zakein*, an elder. This was the way in which they related to Him, because this was the dimension He chose in which to reveal Himself to the world at that point. To say that this was a true representation would be false because Hashem cannot be defined. To define Him would mean attempting to limit His sense of existence to those terms, which cannot be done. Hashem is not limited in any way at all. Thus, when He is perceived in specific ways, it is simply because this is the way He chose to reveal Himself to the *mekabel* at that point, and the *mekabel* is able to relate to Him on those terms. Before we discuss

---

8 *Yirmiyahu* 13:17.

9 5b.

the concept referred to in the *pesukim* as "Hashem crying," let us first explain the idea of *bechiyah*.

Unfortunately, we know all too well the situations in which we are brought to tears. Tears themselves played a role in the *churban*, by the fact that Chazal refer to them as the cause for the destruction of the Beis Hamikdash. As a result of the false words and *lashon harah* of the *meraglim*, the nation cried. Chazal explain that since they cried on the night of Tishah B'Av in vain, Hashem would give them a legitimate reason to cry on that night: the *churban Beis Hamikdash*. In the incident of the *meraglim*, their crying indicated that they did not consider their connection to Eretz Yisrael the essence of their lives, but rather something that would negate it. Tears are what a person expresses when he senses, to some extent, his demise. Because that night they cried for nothing, Hashem provided them with an actual situation in which their existence was indeed challenged. The *Maharal* discusses this idea of tears with regard to Moshe Rabbeinu.

The Gemara in *Masechta Bava Basra*[10] discusses who wrote the last few *pesukim* of the Torah. The *pasuk* says: "And Moshe, Hashem's servant, died there, in the land of Moav, by the mouth of Hashem." How could Moshe have written that he died? One interpretation is that the last *pesukim* were written by Yehoshua, the *talmid* of Moshe. The Gemara gives another interpretation that, indeed, Moshe himself wrote it, "*b'demah*." The *Maharal* explains that *b'demah* means he wrote it while he was crying. Moshe was able to write that he died because in a sense he did; when one cries, he is relating to and in a semi-state of death. The words of the Torah saying that Moshe died can therefore be understood as referring to his recognition of his imminent demise and the sense of death he felt then as a result. Thus, tears represent a form of death, and this relates to what one can perceive in terms of the Presence of Hashem.

Klal Yisrael's entire sense of existence is based upon their spiritual capacity to relate to and serve Hashem. Klal Yisrael is said to be totally

---

10 15a.

alive when their spiritual bond and relationship is at its ultimate level. When their spiritual life isn't secure, their resulting sense of being is compromised as well. This limited sense of being is represented through tears. When Hashem reveals Himself to B'nei Yisrael as crying, it is because B'nei Yisrael at that point can only relate to Hashem in terms of their limited degree of spirituality, which serves as the foundation for the level of life they are then privy to. They can perceive the level of "Hashem crying" because their diminished stature cannot totally relate to perceiving Hashem on a higher level—for everything is revealed in terms of what the *mekabel* can accept and absorb.

When the gates of *tefillah* are closed, the gate that allows the tears of Klal Yisrael to enter is always open. The *gematria* of the word *bechi* is thirty-two, which is the same as the *gematria* of the word *lev*. When we pray, we attempt to be sincere. When we cry, the true feelings of our hearts are being openly revealed. Such prayers enter directly and represent the true sincerity that is the *lev* of the members of Klal Yisrael. We too are crying and, as we say in the *Selichos* in the *piyut* of *Salachti* on the night of Yom Kippur: "Hear my voice and see the tears of my eye, take up my grievance, attend to my words and answer me, I have forgiven." May Hashem hear the sound of our tears during these days when we need *rachamei Shamayim*.

We have focused on the concept of prayer. Interestingly, as important as prayer is, it isn't always the answer. When Klal Yisrael was being chased by the army of Mitzrayim before *krias Yam Suf*, Moshe davened, but Hashem said that at that point he should not have been praying. Why not? Isn't prayer a good thing?

This question is based upon the *pasuk* in *Parashas Beshalach*: "Hashem said to Moshe, '*Mah titzak Elai*...—Why do you cry out to me? Speak to B'nei Yisrael and let them move on.'"[11] *Rashi* explains that from this *pasuk* we learn that Moshe was standing in *tefillah* when Hashem said to him that now is not the time to pray. As the *Chazon Ish* writes in his

11 *Shemos* 14:15.

Igros, tefillah is the mighty stick, the weapon of a person. If so, why were they not to pray at that point? The *Maharal* in *Gevuros Hashem* deals with this issue.

When things exist within a certain framework and there is a desire to change that framework, one prays. The *Maharal* explains to us that B'nei Yisrael were running from the army of Mitzrayim and were faced with the sea before them, with nowhere to go. The state they were in was seemingly one of danger, their very lives were being threatened, and what they needed was a miracle—for the water to split. They perceived themselves as in a problematic situation, and as a result, they prayed. It was at this point that Hashem said, "*Mah titzak Elai*?...let them move on."

The *Maharal* continues to explain that the situation they perceived they needed—that the water should split, which served as the very reason for their prayer—was a sense of reality that already existed in creation. Hashem had been dealing with B'nei Yisrael up to that point within a system of *nissim*. The *pasuk* in the beginning of *Parashas Beshalach* states: "Hashem traveled before them by day in a pillar of cloud to lead their way, and by night in a pillar of fire to provide them with light."[12] Hashem was already dealing with them in miraculous ways, and as such, all they had to do was to travel, and they would be subject to the same state of miracles as before. In a sense, it was as if they had already prayed and Hashem answered them with a resounding yes. Thus, there was no need for them to pray at that point. As a result, Hashem was telling them that *tefillah* wasn't necessary; what they were trying to establish through their prayer was already here.

There is an additional aspect to this. Klal Yisrael required the splitting of the sea in order for their lives to be saved; the water would have to split to enable dry land to be revealed for them to pass through. The *pasuk* in *Parashas Bereishis* says: "Hashem said, 'Let the waters beneath the heavens be gathered into one place, and let the dryness be seen.'"[13] The *Maharal* writes that just as the *yesod* of *avir*, air, surrounds the whole

12 Ibid., 13:21.

13 *Bereishis* 1:9.

world, so too, the *yesod* of *mayim*, water, should be atop of all the land of the earth. Hashem changed what should have been—water over all the top of the earth—in order to give Adam HaRishon the ability to exist. Adam wasn't just another creation; he possessed the *Maaleh Elokis*, the spiritual quality from Hashem that serves as the foundation of why Hashem created His world. The physical world in itself doesn't reflect spirituality, but through the Presence of Hashem, which is pumped into the universe through *avodah*, the goal of revealing His Shechinah in a lowly physical realm can be achieved. But then Adam sinned.

The connection to Hashem and the ultimate purpose of existence couldn't be attained through Adam and his descendants in their spiritually corrupt state. As mentioned previously, someone would have to inherit the fulfillment of the spiritual destiny of Adam, and through his children, the world would become complete. The name of that person was Avraham Avinu, and Klal Yisrael was to be considered the new Adam of the *briah*.

The *Maharal* explains that, at birth, all fetuses are brought forth from the water—the fluid that envelopes them from where the child is born. Similarly, at *krias Yam Suf*, Klal Yisrael represents the birth and creation of the new Adam in terms of being brought forth from water. Faced with the sea before them, they needed its waters to recede and enable the dry land to appear. The *yesod* of *mayim* was already limited to enable the appearance of the dry land in terms of Adam HaRishon, who was originally supposed to perfect the world. Thus, when Klal Yisrael required the same physical reality, the *yesod* of *mayim* was poised to split to enable the continued existence of the new Adam bearing the *Maaleh Elokis*—Klal Yisrael.

Tefillah is a primary vehicle for our connection with Hashem. It is through this that what we need is brought into existence in the world, enabling us to glean what we require as a *mekabel* from the ultimate *Nosein*. But in this case, what we needed was already here; it was previously established as part of the fiber of creation and, as the *Maharal* explains, it did not require *tefillah*. Therefore, B'nei Yisrael standing in prayer at the sea led to Hashem saying to Moshe, "*Mah titzak Elai*...let them move on."

From what occurred at *krias Yam Suf*, we can see that the creation of Klal Yisrael began amid open *nissim*. This system has not ended, but rather it serves as the basis for the Yom Tov of Chanukah.

One of the *berachos* we recite when we kindle the *neiros Chanukah* is, "Blessed are You, Hashem our G-d, King of the universe, *she'asah nissim*—Who has wrought miracles for our forefathers, in those days at this season." One would assume that the *nissim* the *berachah* refers to are those that occurred years ago when the Chashmona'im led Klal Yisrael against the Yevanim and served as the catalyst for the salvation that Hashem brought for B'nei Yisrael. But the *Sefas Emes* adds an additional appreciation to the specific miracles being referenced in the *berachah*, and this may also help us understand the words of the *Ramban* in the beginning of *Parashas Behaloscha*.

Chazal reveal that Aharon HaKohen was upset because he and his *shevet* had not played a role in the *chanukas HaMizbei'ach*, when the Altar was inaugurated through the *korbanos* brought by the *nesi'im*, the heads of each tribe. Hashem told him not to be upset because his mitzvah was to be greater than theirs, as he was to light and clean the *neiros* of the *Menorah*. The *Ramban* in his *peirush* in the beginning of *Parashas Behaloscha* wonders why it was this specific service that soothed Aharon. First, there were other parts to the *avodah* in the *Mishkan* he would also perform, and second, one would assume that when, in the future, there would be no *Mizbei'ach* upon which to offer *korbanos*, there would be no *Menorah* to kindle the *neiros* as well. How was what Aharon was granted better than what the *nesi'im* were granted? The *Ramban* answers that here the Torah is alluding to the "Chanukah" of his children, the Chashmona'im, who would be instrumental in bringing salvation to Klal Yisrael. Through the *Sefas Emes*, we can appreciate the depth of the words of the *Ramban*.

The Gemara in *Masechta Shabbos*[14] reveals the details of what occurred during the era of the Second Beis Hamikdash. The Yevanim entered the Beis Hamikdash and spiritually defiled all of the oil intended for the

---

14 21b.

lighting of the *Menorah* in the Beis Hamikdash. After the Chashmona'im were able to emerge victorious in their war with the Yevanim, they entered the Beis Hamikdash and only found one flask of oil that was sealed by the Kohen Gadol, enough oil to burn for only one day. A *neis* occurred, and it burned for eight days, at which point they were able to produce additional ritually pure *shemen*. The specific *neiros* of the *Menorah* that were kindled during those days when the *neis* of Chanukah occurred reveal the inner dimension of what the *neiros* actually represent.

According to the natural rules of the physical world, there was no way the *Menorah* of the Beis Hamikdash should have been able to burn after the war. Although the physical Beis Hamikdash stood and the *Menorah* actually existed at that point, there was not enough oil for it to physically burn within the confines of our physical world. Yet it did burn, for its capacity to burn was a function of a *neis*. Hashem created *teva*, the nature within which His world exists. The concept of a miracle represents the point at which Hashem is willing to change the *teva* specifically for a singular person or group to reveal the profound and vibrant relationship He has with those who are the recipients of the *neis*. Thus, its actual burning was solely the function of a *neis*. It is this aspect that is present even today in the *neiros* we light for Chanukah.

Unfortunately, today, we have no Beis Hamikdash and no *Menorah*. Although we do possess *shemen*, it is not pure as is required for the lighting of the *Menorah* of the Beis Hamikdash. Yet, the *Sefas Emes* explains that the *Menorah* of the Beis Hamikdash burns in our homes when we light our *neiros Chanukah*. During the eight days of the original miracle, when only one flask of *shemen* was found, the *Menorah* burned through a *neis* because there wasn't enough oil. On the Yom Tov of Chanukah, the *Menorah* of the Beis Hamikdash burns at our doors and windows through an active *neis* as well. We have no Beis Hamikdash, no *Menorah*, and no proper oil, yet the ***Menorah* of the Beis Hamikdash** burns through the great *neis* that occurs nowadays on each of the eight nights of Chanukah. This is what enables the *berachah* of *She'asah nissim*.

Upon seeing the *neiros Chanukah*, one is not merely seeing a vehicle that reminds us of a *neis* that once occurred; the person is actually witnessing the burning of the *Menorah* of the Beis Hamikdash now burning through a *neis* once again. Thus, through the *berachah* of *She'asah Nissim*, in our seeing the *neiros Chanukah*, we are actually witnessing the burning of the *Menorah* of the Beis Hamikdash. Here lies Hashem's appeasement to Aharon, referred to in the words of the *Ramban*.

Theoretically, with the *churban Beis Hamikdash*, just as the *avodah* of sacrificing the *korbanos* upon the *Mizbei'ach* could not continue, so too would Aharon's *avodah* of kindling the *Menorah* cease. But in the *neis* of the victory over the Yevanim, Aharon's descendants, the Chashmona'im, created a system through which the *Menorah* of the Beis Hamikdash would continue to burn. Through our lighting of the *neiros* in our households on Chanukah, the *avodah* of the *Menorah* can survive beyond the days in which the physical structure of the Beis Hamikdash actually stands. The end of the *berachah* of *She'asah nissim* is, "In those days at this season," for that is exactly what occurs. The *neis* of the burning of the *Menorah* that existed during the days when the Beis Hamikdash stood "in those days" once again exists "in these days" as well. When one sees the *neiros Chanukah* burning, one is actually witnessing the performance of a *neis* from Hashem.

Just as we were born as a nation through an openly revealed miracle, so too, we live a *neis* each year at *hadlakas neiros* on the Yom Tov of Chanukah. We were created to live beyond the physical confines of our world of *teva*. "*Ba'yamim ha'heim b'zman ha'zeh*—For what happened in those days is happening again in this time at this season."

The Horn of an Ox

A UNIQUE and quite surprising aspect of the Greek conquest of Eretz Yisrael was their demand that the Jews write "*al keren ha'shor*—on the horn of an ox" that they have no "*chelek b'Elokei Yisrael*—part in the G-d of Yisrael."

What were the Yevanim aiming to achieve by this?

The Yom Tov of Chanukah represents the time that Klal Yisrael emerged victorious from their battle with the Yevanim—the Greeks and their Hellenist supporters—who had attempted to destroy our connection to Hashem and His Torah.

Each of the *Dalet Malchiyos*, the Four Kingdoms that attempted to destroy Klal Yisrael, represented a specific approach in terms of their attack against us. The attack of the Kingdom of Yavan centered upon destroying the spiritual relationship between Klal Yisrael and Hashem. It was not surprising that they, therefore, prohibited the learning of Torah. It is also not surprising that they did not destroy the Beis Hamikdash, but rather proceeded to profane it. They weren't against the building per se—they were against the *kedushah* it housed. With this idea in mind, we will attempt to understand the intent of what is, at first glance, perhaps the most obscure of Yavan's decrees.

They commanded Klal Yisrael: "*Kisvu al keren ha'shor...*—Write upon the horn of an ox that you [Klal Yisrael] have no part in the G-d of Yisrael." Through casual observation, we would not perceive the full intent of this decree and what the Yevanim desired to achive through it.

What is the significance of writing on the horn of an ox, and what did they want to convey? We can understand their motivations, to a certain extent, in their other evil decrees. But why this? The *Maharal* in *Ner Mitzvah* discusses this point.

The antagonism that Yavan bears against Klal Yisrael is not merely one of hatred, but also includes a form of jealousy. The Babylonians didn't necessarily consider themselves worthy of any form of connection with Hashem; they were against the bond B'nei Yisrael had with the Creator. The Yevanim were unique in that they too stood for a form of virtue; they too were considered men of *chochmah* and pursued the delights provided by one's intellect. Their bond to the *chochmah* of the physical world—*teva*—was so intense that they negated any other *chochmah*, including Torah, as being real. In their eyes, any knowledge that could not be proven lacked credibility. Of course, Torah as concepts of right and wrong—what relates to Hashem and what doesn't—cannot be proven within the walls of a sanitized laboratory. They attempted to negate Klal Yisrael as the true bearers of *chochmah*, and thus the children of Avraham, Yitzchak, and Yaakov would thereby be unworthy of a connection with Him. The *Maharal* explains that the decree to write upon the horn of an ox was intended to prove this point: that B'nei Yisrael have no true bond with Hashem.

The *pasuk* in *Tehillim* states: "They exchanged their glory for the likeness of a *shor*—an ox eating grass."[1]

Why upon the horn of a *shor*? The Yevanim wanted B'nei Yisrael to acknowledge that within the midst of *Matan Torah*, directly after *krias Yam Suf*, they had sinned through *avodah zarah* with the *Eigel Ha'Zahav*, the Golden Calf. Yavan's logic was that what occurs during one's inception reflects the true nature and quality of that person or group. The sad fact that the Jews sinned with the Golden Calf—the young *shor*—directly after becoming a nation, proved that Klal Yisrael wasn't truly connected to Hashem and thus weren't worthy of a true relationship with Him. The Yevanim claimed that *they* warranted that

1 *Tehillim* 106:20.

bond, for they were the true bearers and promoters of *chochmah*. Thus, the Yevanim decreed that Klal Yisrael must write upon the horn of a *shor* that they aren't worthy of any connection to Hashem because of the *cheit* of the *eigel*. Along these lines, the *Avnei Nezer* elaborates upon another of the decrees of Yavan against B'nei Yisrael.

The Greeks declared that any woman who was to be married must first be subjected to the *hegmon*, the general. How are we to understand this? Clearly, the Greeks were immoral, but why was this decree a mainstay of their attack? They were engaged in a philosophical and theological war with us, not just giving in to their base natures. How does this decree fit in as part of their arsenal?

The *Avnei Nezer* cites the Gemara in *Masechta Shabbos*[2] that says: "*Aluvah*...—Shameless is the bride who acts unfaithful amid her marriage ceremony." The Gemara is teaching us that this is how the actions of B'nei Yisrael may be considered. In the midst of their marriage with Hashem at *Matan Torah*, they too acted unfaithful and sought the *avodah zarah* of the Golden Calf. Within these terms, the *Avnei Nezer* explains the decree of being subjected to the *hegmon*.

In other words, both these decrees were reminders that we had been unfaithful, and therefore we are not the bearers of a special relationship with Hashem.

The attack of Yavan against B'nei Yisrael was based upon their desire to negate any bond B'nei Yisrael was privileged to have with Hashem, which they felt B'nei Yisrael forfeited due to their sinning with the *Eigel*. They believed that no legitimate bond could possibly ensue if it was premised upon such an act. This, too, was their intent by defying the *kedushah* of the Jewish family. The Yevanim hoped that by subjecting the wife-to-be to such a decree, they would theoretically negate her capacity to develop her total bond with her husband. The decree to write upon the horn of an ox would serve to validate Yavan's claim that B'nei Yisrael are not to be considered Hashem's nation. The decree to be subjected to the *hegmon* solidified that view. Klal Yisrael was to be considered as

2 88b.

one who acted unfaithfully during her *chuppah*, with that affecting her relationship with Hashem; therefore, all the Jewish brides would be considered accordingly, and this would prevent them from developing the proper bonds with their husbands.

However, the Yevanim were mistaken. The *pasuk* in *Yeshayah* reveals our true sense of connection with Hashem: "Can a woman forget her baby, or not feel mercy for the child of her womb?"[3] Although on the one hand, many of the customs of bride and groom are learned from what occurred at *Matan Torah* between Hashem and Klal Yisrael, the *Maharal* explains that the bond we share with Hashem is also considered one of a parent to a child. Whatever challenges the relationship between *ish v'ishah* may be subjected to, the bond of parent to child is **not** subject to being nullified. This bond is secure and there is no possibility of it ever being removed. Our connection to Hashem therefore exists *l'netzach*, for ultimately, we are considered as "*banim l'Makom*," and as children, we possess a bond that is eternal.

As the *Maharal* states many times throughout his *sefarim*: "*Devarim gedolim einam b'mikrah*—Great things are not merely coincidence." The fact that it was specifically the Yevanim who demanded of B'nei Yisrael to write on the horn of an ox that they have no "*chelek b'Elokei Yisrael*" means it reflects the essence of the specific attack that the Yevanim waged against Klal Yisrael. The *Maharal*, in his *sefer Ner Mitzvah*, explains what that specific attack was. To understand this idea more clearly, we need some background.

Regarding the *avodah* of the Kohen Gadol during his performance on Yom Kippur in the *Kodesh HaKadoshim*, the *pasuk* in *Parashas Acharei Mos* says: "He [the Kohen] shall take some of the blood of the bull and sprinkle with his finger, above the surface of the Ark-cover...and before the Ark-cover he shall sprinkle some blood with his finger seven times. He shall slaughter the he-goat sin-offering that belongs to the

3 *Yeshayah* 49:15.

people...He shall do with its blood just as he did with the blood of the bull."[4]

Rashi explains that the Kohen was required to sprinkle the blood of the goat "*achas l'maalah v'sheva l'matah*"—once upward above the *kapores*, cover, and seven times downward below it. The Gemara in *Masechta Yoma* teaches us that he would actually count one, one and one, one and two, until finally he would count one and seven. This specific way of counting demonstrates that the one sprinkle above and seven sprinkles below are to be considered as two separate units, for through those sprinkles, the exalted Klal Yisrael is being established as being spiritually higher than the rest of the nations of the world.

The *Maharal* explains that there are two distinct worlds or realms of reality:

- The world of *teva*, depicting the physical world we live in of *Olam Hazeh*, is a function of the seven days, as well as the various cycles of seven—e.g., the years of *Shemittah*—present within it.
- The realm that will be revealed at the conclusion of this world is the spiritual realm of reward of *Olam Haba*. Although it will only actually be revealed after our world, it serves as the source and reason as to why the world of *Olam Hazeh* was created.

The *Maharal* therefore refers to the realm of *Olam Haba* as the world of "eight" and "*l'maalah min ha'teva*—beyond the world of *teva*," while *Olam Hazeh* is referred to as that of "seven."

The physical world exists to supply Man with the *bechirah* through which he may serve his Creator and earn his reward in the World to Come. In this sense, it is "*sof maaseh b'machshavah techilah*," that which is revealed last within the actual world was the true intent that was thought of initially. Thus, during the *avodah* on Yom Kippur, the Kohen sprinkles the blood of the goat and specifically counts one, one and one, one and two, until finally he counts one and seven. What does this indicate?

---

4 *Vayikra* 16:14.

- The sprinkling of the blood above the *kapores* once reflects the awesome *kedushah* of B'nei Yisrael. The source of their unique holy *neshamah* stems from the world of *l'maalah min ha'teva*, that of "eight."
- The sprinkling of the blood seven times below demonstrates that the nations are subject to an existence grounded in the realm of "seven," the world of *teva*. Their Seven Commandments reflect this point: that their true sense of existence is only within the confines of *Olam Hazeh*.

The blood is the life force of all life, and as the *pasuk* in *Parashas Re'eh* says: "*Ki ha'dam hu ha'nefesh*—The blood is the soul of the being."[5] The essence of the nations of the world is a function of the world of *teva*, and therefore, the sprinkling of seven times below the *kapores* reflects that they are part and parcel of the world of "seven" and that of an imperfect existence in accordance with *cheit.*

Klal Yisrael's essence stems from the world of "eight." This is reflected in the one sprinkling above the *kapores*, which refers to the world beyond *teva*, that of "eight." Thus, Klal Yisrael proclaims that they are truly connected to the spiritual realm and possess an inherent connection to Hashem. As we saw, Yavan claimed that Klal Yisrael's *cheit* of the Golden Calf openly defied the existence of just such a connection.

When someone forms an association with another, the initial style of behavior reflects the true nature of the relationship. After some time, the person might become lax in his commitment, but at least in the initial stage, the person would put their best foot forward. B'nei Yisrael sinned with the Golden Calf at the beginning of their relationship with Hashem, in the midst of *Matan Torah*. Yavan claimed that their actions reflected the true nature of who they are, that they were therefore not the exalted spiritual people who claim to have a connection to Hashem resulting from the spiritual greatness of their soul. As we saw, their demand for B'nei Yisrael to write on the horn of a *shor* was meant to show B'nei Yisrael that the *cheit ha'eigel*—an *eigel* being a young

5 *Devarim* 12:23.

shor—revealed that they weren't special. They attempted to claim that the soul of B'nei Yisrael wasn't a function of the realm of eight at all. It was specifically Yavan that challenged them in just such a way.

In other words, at a deeper level, the battle between Yavan and Klal Yisrael lies in Yavan's denial that the world of seven is in any way connected to the source realm of eight—that of *Olam Haba*. They view the physical world as its own entity that exists purely for the physical and deny the presence of a spiritual realm at all. The *gematria* of "Yavan," spelled with the letters of *yud*, *vav*, and *nun*, is sixty-six, that of the word *galgal* (*gimmel-lamed-gimmel-lamed*). The word *galgal* means "circle," which is something that is totally contained within itself. While a square is a function of parallel lines that never connect with each other and exist beyond the square itself, each point of a circle leads to the next to complete the entire circle as a closed unit. This was the claim of Yavan: that this world exists for the pursuit of the physical alone.

But Klal Yisrael believes that the world of *teva* is born from the world of eight, and as such, is directly connected to the realm of *kedushah* and Hashem. It is the Yom Tov of Chanukah that reflects this point.

In the *Maoz Tzur*, the song of Chanukah, we sing: "Yevanim gathered against me then in the days of the Chashmona'im. They broke down the walls of my towers, and they spiritually defiled all the oils; and from the one remnant of the flasks, a miracle was done for the roses [B'nei Yisrael]. Men of insight established days of eight for song and jubilation."

Chanukah is not merely a holiday that "happens to be" eight days long. Rather, during these days, the world of eight is revealed openly and may be perceived within the world of seven. The word *shemen*, oil, is from the word *shemoneh*, eight, for locked up within the *shemen* is the holy realm represented in the pure *ohr* that is the *shoresh* of our physical existence. It is this point that a strict translation of the words of *Maoz Tzur* is conveying. It doesn't say that "*b'nei binah*—men of insight" established "*shemonah yamim*—eight days" for song and jubilation, but rather, "*yemei shemonah*—days of eight," for such is the true spiritual flavor of the Yom Tov of Chanukah. They are "days of eight," where the *kedushah* of the metaphysical world of *Olam Haba* is perceived as the *shoresh* of the physical realm of *Olam Hazeh*.

The Yevanim demanded that we denounce our connection to Hashem, but of course that is impossible, for we are so closely connected. We are a "nation of eight," who light the *ohr* of the *Menorah* in a physical world during the "days of eight" of Chanukah.

As we saw, the *Maharal* in *Ner Mitzvah* explains that the Yevanim wanted Klal Yisrael to write on the horn of a *shor* to show that as a result of the *cheit ha'eigel*, Klal Yisrael wasn't connected to Hashem. The Yevanim claimed that had Klal Yisrel truly been privy to a strong and deep relationship with Hashem, it would not have been possible for them to succumb to such a severe *cheit* at the beginning of their nationhood. We saw this above.

The *Shelah HaKadosh* explains their insistence on the *keren* of the *shor* in a different fashion.

Man is called "Adam" as a result of two qualities that he possesses. One reflects his exalted greatness, while the other is his potential for lowliness:

- Due to man's exalted spiritual soul, he possesses the ability to be "*adameh l'Elyon*—similar to the One Above." Man is unique in that he is composed of a spiritual soul which gives him the capacity to relate to his Creator for all eternity.
- Man can also sink to the lowest point of existence and bring down his world as well. His name "Adam" reflects this potential, as he is created from the *adamah*, the earth of the ground we tread upon.

Thus, Man has it in him to go either way: to soar and connect with *tov* or fall and bond with *ra*. These two possibilities in Man were reflected in his two states: first, in the initial creation of Adam HaRishon; and second, after he sinned by eating from the forbidden fruit of the *Eitz Ha'daas*.

The *pasuk* that ends *Parashas Ki Sisa* states: "When B'nei Yisrael saw Moshe's face, *ki karan ohr pnei Moshe*—that Moshe's face became radiant, Moshe put the mask back on his face."[6] In our terms, the *keren*, horn, of light that radiated from Moshe's face reflected that his physical sense of being was **totally** negated by his spiritual dimension. Thus, what was projected from his *panim*, face, the place in the *tzuras Adam* that reveals the inner being, the *pnim*, of the person, was the sense of *ohr* that defined his holy *neshamah*. Adam HaRishon, prior to his *cheit* with the *Eitz Ha'daas*, radiated light, as the *pasuk* in *Chavakuk* says: "A glow was like the light, *karnayim*—rays of light, came from His hand to him."[7] This state, where *karnayim*, beacons of light, are radiated from the person, represents Man's ideal state of being and what existed *kodem ha'cheit*. In that state, Man's label of "Adam" was based upon his capacity to be *adameh l'Elyon*. In that state, the clarity of *Hashem Echad* is being projected from man's *etzem* in that his *guf* exists purely to serve his *neshamah*. It is the *keren* of *ohr* that reveals this posture of the ideal man recognizing the absolute Sovereignty of Hashem. But after his *cheit*, he had descended to something merely created from the dirt of the ground—*adamah*. Yet, even in that state, Adam HaRishon attempted to recognize that, indeed, Hashem is *Echad*.

The *Maharsha* explains the Gemara in *Masechta Chulin*,[8] which says that **after** Adam HaRishon had sinned, he brought a *shor* with only one horn as an offering to Hashem.

In our terms, we understand that although he had sinned and seemed to portray a posture that, *chalilah*, there is another will in creation besides that which reflects the *Ratzon Hashem*, Adam was attempting to proclaim that there is indeed only One Hashem. This statement was reflected through the ox with only one horn. Thus, while Adam himself couldn't project the *keren* of *ohr* because he himself had sinned, he accepted that the absolute unity of Hashem could be presented through his offering of a *shor*. Adam, in a sense, had lost the *madreigah* of *adameh l'Elyon*, with its *keren* of *ohr*, and within his lowly stature of representing *adamah*—through the *shor* that possessed but one *keren*—he could still

---

6 *Shemos* 34:29.

7 *Chavakuk* 3:4.

8 60a.

essentially proclaim that there is One G-d, Hashem. Yavan's attack was focused upon challenging this spiritual statement.

The *pasuk* in *Daniel* proclaims with regard to the nation of Yavan: "And the he-goat had a noticeable horn between its eyes."[9] The *Shelah* explains that the *keren* of Yavan serves as the spiritually impure contrast to the ultimate *keren* of *ohr* that was originally projected by Adam HaRishon before the *cheit*. Yavan didn't destroy the physical building that served as the Beis Hamikdash but destroyed its *kedushah* and didn't allow its spirituality to project from its physical dimension. The Yevanim therefore insisted that the Jewish Nation write on the *keren* of a *shor* that they are not connected to Hashem in order to wage their war with B'nei Yisrael's sense of spirituality. As a result of the *Cheit Ha'eigel*, B'nei Yisrael had lost the spiritual dimension they had attained when they stood at Har Sinai, at which point the results of the spiritual catastrophe of the *cheit* of Adam HaRishon had ceased. In that secondary state, just as Adam had brought the *shor* with one horn on its head, so too B'nei Yisrael were able to exist within that diminished spiritual dimension as well. It was with the goal to eradicate that spiritual capacity that Yavan attacked.

The Yevanim demanded that B'nei Yisrael write upon the horn of a *shor*—Adam HaRishon's vehicle to admit the Oneness of Hashem after he sinned—and B'nei Yisrael would thereby admit that they themselves were far removed even from that level of *kedushah*. It was therefore upon the horn of the ox that the focus of their antagonism was based when they decreed, "*Kisvu al keren ha'shor she'ein lachem chelek b'Elokei Yisrael.*"

The idea that B'nei Yisrael are forever seeking the *ohr* of *adameh l'Elyon* is also reflected in the *minhag* to gaze at one's fingernails from the flame of Havdalah, clearly stated in the *Shulchan Aruch*.[10] What is the meaning of this *minhag*?

The *pasuk* in *Parashas Bereishis* states: "And Hashem Elokim made for Adam and his wife *kasnos ohr* (the word *ohr* is spelled with the letter

---

9 *Daniel* 8:5.

10 *Orach Chaim* 298:3.

ayin)—coats of skin, and He clothed them."[11] *Rashi* explains that the clothes were as smooth as fingernails attached to their skin. In our terms, Chazal discuss that Rabbi Meir had a *Sefer Torah* in which the words *kasenos ohr* spelled the word *ohr* with the letter *alef* instead of *ayin. Ohr* with an *ayin* means "leather" or "skin," while *ohr* spelled with an *alef* means "light."

As was mentioned earlier, the *Shelah Hakadosh* explains that Adam HaRishon was created *b'Tzelem Elokim*, in the image of Hashem. He was created with a *guf* formed from the ground and a *neshamah*, which is referred to by Chazal as a *chelek Elokei mi'maal*, a *chelek* of Hashem. Adam was called by that name because he was created from the *adamah*. But the additional implication that lies in the name of Adam is in his ultimate capacity to be *adameh l'Elyon*, similar to Hashem in heaven. In his relationship to pure spirituality, Adam's *guf* was not to be considered a separate entity from his *neshamah*. Rather, it was to totally serve his soul and be the vehicle and mechanism for a purely spiritual entity—the soul—to have the capacity to exist within the framework of a physical world. In the world of Adam HaRishon prior to when he sinned by eating from the fruit of the *Eitz Ha'daas*, his *guf* was *ohr*—not with an *ayin*, meaning mere skin, but with an *alef*, implying light. Before he sinned, Adam's *guf* was subservient to his soul and as such revealed the spiritual splendor of his *neshamah* to an external world. His external shell shone brightly the *ohr* that was an expression of the spiritual light of his soul. Thus, his *ohr* was *ohr* with an *alef*.

But then he sinned. Once again, in our terms, his *cheit* represented that his physical dimension wasn't purely in terms of his soul—*adameh l'Elyon*—but it exists with its own sense of an agenda. It is created from the ground, *adamah*, and is therefore a separate entity from his spiritual soul. In stark contrast to *ohr* with an *alef*, his external shell now became *ohr* with an *ayin*—meaning mere skin. The word *ohr* with an *ayin* is spelled with the letters of *ayin*, *vav*, and *reish*. Those letters also spell *eiver*, one who is blind, as in the *pasuk*: "*Lifnei eiver*—Before a

---

11 *Bereishis* 3:21.

blind person you should not place a stumbling block."[12] His mere skin represents that it is totally **blind** from perceiving the true light that emanates from his soul. In our *Sefer Torah*, the word *ohr* in *kasenos ohr* is spelled with an *ayin*, for ultimately, we live in the world that is post the *cheit* of Adam. But the midrash is also indicating that Rabbi Meir's *Sefer Torah* referred to the *kasenos ohr* of Adam as in some way retaining its exalted level of *ohr* with an *alef*. Although we don't read from the Torah of Rabbi Meir, Havdalah serves as a time when we can somewhat relate to this level.

Rav Tzadok explains that if one would purely look in terms of the *pesukim* depicting the first seven days of creation, one would assume that the *cheit* of Adam occurred **after** Shabbos. But such was not the case. Adam and Chavah sinned on that Friday, Erev Shabbos. Although the world that the first Shabbos entered was post-*cheit*, the *kedushah* of Shabbos is beyond *cheit* and in a sense not affected by it. In his *kuntres Kedushas Shabbos*, Rav Tzadok writes that the *neshamah yeseirah*, the added soul a member of Klal Yisrael is *zocheh* to receive on Shabbos, is the sense of *kedushah* of Adam HaRishon's soul before he sinned. Shabbos is "*me'ein Olam Haba*," a glimmer of the realm of reward that Hashem has given to our physical world. In the world of reward, there is no sense of *cheit*, for evil only exists in the physical domain of *avodah*, where we are to be challenged by it and decide with our *bechirah* whether to serve Hashem or not. Therefore, when the *cheit* is discussed in the Torah, it is only mentioned after Shabbos. This connects to our question regarding the *minhag* to look at one's fingernails during Havdalah.

We are reciting Havdalah and leaving the awesome *kedushah* of the realm prior to the *cheit*. In the world before the *cheit*, the external shell of Adam was *ohr* with an *alef*. It revealed the spiritual splendor and light of his holy *neshamah*. As *Rashi* explains, in some sense, the *kasenos ohr* were attached to Adam and Chavah in a similar manner to one's fingernails. *Sefarim* explain that the *minhag* is therefore to view the light of the Havdalah candle in our fingernails. The *kasenos ohr* were similar

---

12 *Vayikra* 19:14.

to fingernails, so when we see the *ohr* in our fingernails, we once again experience the state of *kasenos ohr* with an *alef.* And although Shabbos is leaving, we acknowledge that the sense of that true reality was able to exist. For once again, our external shell radiates *ohr*.

At one point, mankind possessed that great *ohr*, and it is the spiritual destiny of Klal Yisrael as the new "Adam" of the *briah* to be *zocheh* to it once again. But it was the Yevanim who challenged that *ohr*.

As we saw, the *Maharal* explains that the Yevanim understood from the fact that B'nei Yisrael had sinned by serving the *Eigel Ha'Zahav* that they weren't the true bearers of a connection with Hashem. They interpreted the fact that in the midst of receiving Hashem's Torah, B'nei Yisrael were able to sin, which meant that the bond that should have been forged obviously had not. The *Maharal* adds a specific dimension to this point.

Unfortunately, even though a person truly intends to stay the course and commit himself to *avodas Hashem*, as time passes, those initial sincere feelings start to wane. Thus, the true seeker of Hashem must constantly reinvigorate his devotion to Hashem in order to keep it alive and vibrant. But what of one who loses their enthusiasm not from the course of time, but in the initial stages of his quest? Would this mean that his basic sense of commitment was faulty?

It was regarding this point that the Yevanim challenged B'nei Yisrael's relationship with Hashem.

Directly after Klal Yisrael became a nation at *yetzias Mitzrayim*, having been redeemed from their bondage in Mitzrayim, and now poised at Har Sinai to receive Hashem's Torah, they sinned by serving the Golden Calf. Whichever way we understand how such great people could have violated such a severe *cheit* as idol worship, the fact remains that in some capacity, the nation did succumb. It wasn't later in their history, but in their infant stage, which seems to suggest that their true nature was to not be totally connected to Hashem. This incident seems to challenge their capacity to be the bearers of a "*chelek* of Hashem" and for this to be embedded deep within their collective soul. The Yevanim used this point to challenge B'nei Yisrael.

Why were they wrong?

The *Maharal* answers as follows. The *Aseres HaDibros*—which reveal Hashem's Eternal Will to B'nei Yisrael—start with the words, "*Anochi Hashem Elokecha...*—I am Hashem your G-d, Who has taken you out of the land of Mitzrayim, from the house of slavery." The *Maharal* points out that the word "therefore" is not used—that **because** Hashem took us out of Mitzrayim, we are **therefore** expected to serve Him and be His nation. Rather, Hashem established, for all eternity, that He is our G-d—no matter what we do or how we act. It was as if Hashem established that bond with us without any input from us; thus, our subsequent actions have no relevance in testifying to the validity of the bond. Even in terms of B'nei Yisrael's acceptance of the Torah, it wasn't truly considered as B'nei Yisrael playing their role by "choosing" to accept the Torah as a result of a thought-out decision. Usually, when a person decides, he weighs his options and then decides; but such was not the case at *Kabalas Ha'Torah*. They had said, "*Naaseh v'nishma*," which meant that they totally absolved their own sense of self and choice in their willingness to become One with the Creator. The *Maharal* adds that since this was a blanket acceptance of *Ratzon Hashem*, rather than the result of carefully deciding about each of the mitzvos, they weren't considered as equal players in terms of the establishment of the relationship. The *Maharal*, in his *sefer Ohr Chadash*, compares what happened at Har Sinai with the law of an *anusah*, when a man forces a woman immorally and attacks her.

The *pasuk* in *Parashas Ki Seitzei* says regarding one who forcibly attacks a single woman: "The man...shall give the father of the girl fifty silver [*shekalim*], and she shall become his wife, because he had afflicted her; he cannot divorce her for all his life."[13] The *Maharal* explains that when one allows his own will to dominate totally over the wishes of another, as in the case of an *anusah*, he cannot divorce and sever the bond that

---

13 *Devarim* 22:29.

he alone established. Because he acted with such control that, as far as he was concerned, the relationship had to exist—for he was willing to force her—then so be it; that becomes the way he has to relate to her for the rest of his life. This then becomes the eternal *Ratzon Hashem.* The *pasuk* in *Parashas Yisro* states: "And they [the *B'nei Yisrael*] stood *b'sachtis ha'har*—at the bottom of the mountain."[14] Chazal explain that it means they stood under the mountain, for Hashem had hoisted Har Sinai on top of B'nei Yisrael and told them that if they accept the Torah, good, but if not, "*Sham tehei kevuraschem*—there will be your grave."[15] We were forced to receive the Torah so that we should be considered, as the *Maharal* says, "the *anusim* of Hashem." The revelation of Hashem's Will of "*Anochi Hashem Elokecha*" is that His connection and absolute *ahavah* for us is not dependent upon anything, and it is absolute. It is this powerful message that reveals the folly and *sheker*, falsehood, of the Yevanim who attempted to deny and thereby destroy B'nei Yisrael.

They had wanted us to sign the horn of the ox to proclaim that because of the *Cheit Ha'eigel* we are, *chalilah*, not connected to Hashem. They had wanted us to buy into the *sheker* that denies that within us dwells a *chelek* of Hashem that serves as our *neshamah* and represents our true sense of self and being.

In truth, however, no matter what we do, the soul that beats within us is a *chelek* of Hashem, to the exclusion of any other nation of the world. We possess the *Tzelem Elokim*, and as a result, only we are called "Adam"—and not the nations of the world.

In this sense, the Yom Tov of Chanukah reflects the separation between B'nei Yisrael and the nations of the world. Just as water and oil don't mix, so too B'nei Yisrael and the nations are meant to have no connection, for our connection is only with Hashem through our *neshamah*, a *chelek Elokei mimaal.*

---

14 *Shemos* 19:17.

15 *Masechta Shabbos* 88a.

The Number Eight

THE RAMA IN *Shulchan Aruch* writes that we eat cheese on Chanukah because the *neis* occurred through dairy products.[1] Yehudis, the daughter of Yochanan the Kohen Gadol, gave cheese to the general of the opposing army—together with wine to get him drunk—and was then able to kill him. The enemy then fled, and B'nei Yisrael were able to emerge victorious.

Let us take a look at an additional insight. The *Maharal* in his *sefarim* regularly discusses the *yesod* of the unique relationship between the world of *teva* and the realm of "*l'maalah min ha'teva*—beyond the natural world." The world of *teva* is expressed through the number seven, with seven days of the week, the seven-year *shemittah* cycle, and the seven cycles of *shemittah* that lead to the year of *yovel.* The realm of beyond *teva* is expressed with the number eight. This is actually the source from where the world of seven originates. Thus, the number eight refers to the step before that—in a sense, giving birth to the world of seven. This realm represents absolute *kedushah*, one of total purity and supreme spirituality. The world of eight represents *Olam Haba*, which is the goal we seek throughout our lives in the physical realm of *Olam Hazeh*. This idea represents the foundation of the inherent difference between Klal Yisrael and the Yevanim.

---

1 *Orach Chaim* 670:2.

The Yevanim personified total allegiance to the world of seven and *teva*. Nature and all it entails was the focus of their dedication. One of the main mitzvos they opposed was that of *bris milah*, circumcision, which is performed on the eighth day of a child's life. This mitzvah is performed specifically on the eighth day of the child's life to establish the identity of each member of Klal Yisrael as a person who, while physically existing in the world of seven, has his true domain in the realm of eight, beyond *teva*. The battle of Klal Yisrael and Yavan was to establish the true realm, whether of *teva* or beyond *teva*. Does this world exist for itself or merely to serve and lead to *Olam Haba*? In a somewhat cryptic fashion, the *Maharal* writes that the *gematria* of *heichel*, the Beis Hamikdash building, is sixty-five, while Yavan is sixty-six. Because of that, the Yevanim had initial control over B'nei Yisrael. The *Maharal* reveals to us that Klal Yisrael and their pursuit of *Olam Haba* emerged victorious over the Yevanim because of what was hidden deep within the *Heichel*—the *Kodesh HaKadoshim*, the Holy of Holies.

The word *heichel* is classically spelled with the four letters of *heh*, *yud*, *chaf*, and *lamed*. But the word *heichel* also includes an additional sound, which is buried beneath the letter *heh*, within the sounding of the vowel *tzeirei*. The "*ei*" sound seems to include the letter *yud*, even though in actuality, the letter isn't present in the formal spelling of the word. The *Maharal* explains that it is this "hidden *yud*," buried within *heichel*, that fostered Klal Yisrael's victory. For now, because of the *yud*, the *gematria* of *heichel* became seventy-five—surpassing the sixty-six of Yavan. Obviously, this is not merely in terms of numbers, but that the numbers portray the essence and meaning of the elements involved. The world of *teva* comes from its source of the realm of eight. And it was this quality that was expressed in the innermost chamber of the *heichel*.

The Gemara in *Masechta Berachos*[2] teaches us that David HaMelech dwelled in five different worlds and sang songs of *shirah*, praise, to Hashem about each of them. He dwelled as a fetus in his mother's *rechem*, womb, and sang praises. He was born and emerged into the open

2 10a.

air, and he sang praises. He nursed from his mother and once again sang praises. He sang praises when he nursed because he recognized how Hashem created the specific place where a child nurses from his mother in a different area from the place where a young animal nurses from its mother. An animal feeds its young from the general area where it relieves itself, while a child nurses from the *makom binah*, opposite the place of insight, which is above the mother's *lev*. This is because the sustenance of life must come from the place where the source of life is derived. Thus, the nursing takes place upon *binah she'ba'lev,* the insight of the heart. Chazal teach us that the poles of the *Aron*, which contained the *Luchos Ha'bris*, and was housed in the *Kodesh HaKadoshim*, protruded from the *paroches*, curtain, that separated the two distinct places of the *Heichel*. It separated the outer chamber of the *Heichel*, where the *avodah* took place, and the inner sanctum, where no man but the Kohen Gadol on Yom Kippur was permitted to enter. The poles were to protrude externally to give the appearance of a woman. The outer chamber of the *Heichel* was indeed a holy place, but it represented the ultimate state of *kedushah* of **our** world. The Yevanim were therefore able to negatively affect its *kedushah* and they defiled it. As mentioned previously, the *gematria* of Yavan is sixty-six, while that of *Heichel* is only sixty-five.

But deep inside the *Heichel* was hidden the Holy of Holies. The Torah was there and, as Chazal teach us, it was a place that defied natural law. Physical boundaries and distances weren't the rule in the place where the total spiritual realm of eight was represented in the physical world. The *Kodesh HaKadoshim* was the realm of eight that was the source for all life being pumped into the physical world of seven. Just as nursing occurs above the *binah*, insight, of the heart in a woman, for the nurturing of life emanates from above the place that serves as its source—the heart—so too did that relationship exist in terms of the *Kodesh HaKadoshim* and the *paroches*. The *Kodesh HaKadoshim* serves as the heart with its nurturing capacity represented through the positioning of the poles protruding from the *peroches*. In that totally spiritual realm, the Yevanim had no dominance, and they were thus defeated, for ultimately, the *gematria* of *Heichel* with its hidden dimension, alluded to through the hidden extra letter *yud*, is seventy-five. It is the place where the world of seven—*Heichel*—can be born and nurtured from the world of eight, the *Kodesh HaKadoshim*.

The above idea connects to the eating of dairy on Chanukah. The essence of the *kedushah* of Chanukah lies in the fact that our world is derived from the holy world of *Olam Haba*. This relationship, represented in the two areas of the *Heichel*—the outer part and its innermost chamber of *Kodesh HaKadoshim*—is reflected in the physical structure of Man. The heart reflects the secret of *Olam Haba* and pumps life to the entire being, just like *Olam Haba* gives life and meaning to the physical world. Sustenance—milk and all dairy—are derived from the area above the heart to acknowledge that the *lev* is the true source of life within the person and, therefore, nurturing emanates from there as well. Through dairy we sense that our life emanates from the source that is the *lev*. The salvation and *neis* of Chanukah was from the silent part of *Heichel*, the true source that brings forth the physical realm that corresponds to the heart of Man that enables his actual existence. Chanukah is celebrated for eight days, even though they had enough oil for one day because the first day itself also only exists as a result of the world of eight. Therefore, we eat dairy because through it we portray the essence of the victory of the spiritual Klal Yisrael and their connection to Hashem over the physical Yevanim.

The *Maharal* in *Ner Mitzvah* discusses the significance of the Kohanim in the *yeshuah* brought about against the Yevanim and how it was specifically the *kedushah* of the Kohen Gadol that enabled it to occur. Through the holy and profound words of the *Maharal*, we can begin to appreciate what the battle that Klal Yisrael waged with the Yevanim truly represented. The *Maharal* discusses the *gematria* of the word "Kohen"—*chaf*, *heh*, and *nun* equal seventy-five, which has significance in terms of what the Yevanim were attempting to accomplish against Klal Yisrael.

The battle with Yavan wasn't an external war, but one that challenged the presence of any internal sense of meaning and *kedushah*. The Yevanim stood purely for the external shell; they worshipped the body and the idea that nature created it, establishing it as existing with no sense of spirituality. This explains why they attempted to stop *bris milah*. It wasn't just that they wanted to prevent a mitzvah; they saw *bris milah* as something that challenged the entire premise of Yavan. The basic tenet of the *bris* is that *teva*, the nature that seemingly runs the world, is flawed. If, for example, every child born had to be subjected to the removal of skin upon the ear, a natural outgrowth would be the feeling that *teva* hadn't properly completed the process of birth. The basic nature of the Yevanim abhorred the idea that Man is required to "fix" the process. Here lies the arena of battle between Klal Yisrael and Yavan.

We have learned that the physical world is composed of elements that relate to the number seven. The spiritual realm is reflected by the number eight, and in a sense, gives birth to the world of seven. The *tachlis* is to perceive the Presence of Hashem hidden within the physical world to give it life, similar to the heart, which is hidden and pumps vitality to the total body of the person. The ultimate *Kavod Shamayim*, Honor of Heaven, is revealed only through it being sensed through the veils of a physical shell, while the physical world has no intrinsic value other than as the veil to be pierced. Here lies the battle Yavan waged with B'nei Yisrael.

To Yavan, all that matters is the world of seven. But the *milah* on the eighth day proclaims that Klal Yisrael exists not for the sake of the world of *teva* but for the dimension that stands as its hidden source. The grand battle that is waged occurs between the Yevanim, who live only in the physical realm, and Klal Yisrael, who fervently believe there is meaning and a hidden dimension. The Kohen entered this fight and brought with him the true sense of identity of one whose *gematria* is seventy-five. Seventy-five serves as the midpoint between the realms of seven and eight, depicted in the numbers of seventy and eighty (i.e., seven and eight multiplied by ten). The Kohen's role in *avodah* is to merge worlds, to elevate the world of seven to that of eight, and as such, it was pivotal in the war against the alleged supremacy of the world of seven. But the *Maharal* adds a point that sheds overwhelming light in terms of appreciating this very deep concept.

The Kohen Gadol wore eight garments because he personified the merger effected by the Kohen. The *pasuk* says: "*Shamayim, shamayim l'Hashem*...—Heaven belongs to Hashem, but the earth belongs to Man." [3] One would think that as a result, Man would be permitted to enter all places of the land that indeed do belong to him. But this is not the case. The *Kodesh HaKadoshim* in the Beis Hamikdash was an area on earth that was seemingly off-limits. Only the Kohen Gadol on Yom Kippur was able to enter that place to perform his *avodah* for Klal Yisrael. Chazal reveal to us that the Kohen Gadol was able to enter the *Kodesh HaKadoshim* because of the *kedushah* of the *bris milah*. For it is true, all the land belongs to Man and this enables him to tread upon it, but the *Kodesh HaKadoshim* is not truly part of the earth.

Hashem created the realm of eight—pure heaven—to exist in a sense in this world, to be perceived as the source from where all physical life emanates. The *ohr* of the Torah emerges from the *Kodesh HaKadoshim* to give life to the world. We are not permitted to go there, for it isn't part of the land that was given to us. It is part of heaven, and thus, only the Kohen Gadol who wears eight garments can go in the merit of the *milah* performed on the eighth day. He can enter on the awesome day of Yom Kippur because on the other 364 days of the year, the Satan has the power to promote evil (indeed, the *gematria* of *ha'satan—heh, shin, tes*—and *nun* equals 364), but on this holy day when the world reverts back to the spiritual realm through *teshuvah*, he has no control. On the day when the members of Klal Yisrael are as *malachim*, angels, and not as human beings, the place from the realm of eight is permitted entry.

It is the Kohen Gadol's unique capacity to truly merge the realms, and this facilitated the victory of Klal Yisrael over the Yevanim. It is this idea that is reflected in the song of Chanukah, *Maoz Tzur*, which refers specifically to the *neis* of Chanukah.

The stanza reads, "Yevanim gathered against me then in the days of the Chashmona'im. They broke down the walls of my towers and they spiritually defiled all the oils; and from the one remnant of the flasks

---

3 *Tehillim* 115:16.

a miracle was done for the roses [B'nei Yisrael]. **Men of insight** established **days of eight** for song and jubilation." The miracle that occurred was that they found one flask sealed with the seal of the Kohen Gadol to enable the *shemen* to be used for the mitzvah. *The word shemen* comes from the word *shemoneh*, eight, for the light that is released from within the olive reflects the light of the world of eight. Thus, *b'nei binah*, people of insight, who perceive the external and its inner spiritual mechanism that gives it life as well, established not merely eight days of song, but rather "*yemei shemoneh*—days of eight," when the *kedushah* of the realm of eight is perceived as present within the external shell of the world we live in, serving as its true source. They are indeed days where the realm of eight is revealed to foster song and jubilation. It is where the *ohr* of the *ner Chanukah* is able to bring forth the *ohr* of the realm of *shemoneh* into the darkness that permeates the world of seven—to enable us, even though we stand in the world of seven, to truly dwell in the world of eight.

In light of the above, it is no wonder that the eighth day of Chanukah has a special status. The *pasuk* in *Parashas Vayechi* states: "All these are the tribes of Yisrael, twelve; *v'zos*—and this is what their father spoke to them and he blessed them."[4] Chazal reveal to us that Yaakov imparted to his children, the *Shevatim*, the concept of *zos*, this. There is another instance where this idea is used to explain a state of profound *kedushah*. The last day of Chanukah is referred to as "*Zos Chanukah*," based upon the *pasuk* toward the end of *Parashas Naso*, which states: "*Zos chanukas haMizbei'ach*—This is the dedication of the Altar,"[5] read on the last day of Chanukah. The *Sefas Emes* explains the significance of *zos* and how it relates to Yaakov and to Chanukah. The key to understanding this point lies in the *pesukim* in *Parashas Ki Sisa* that deal with the Golden Calf.

The *pasuk* in *Ki Sisa* says: "He took from their hands and formed it with an engraving tool and made it into a molten calf. They [B'nei

4 *Bereishis* 49:28.

5 *Bamidbar* 7:11.

Yisrael] said, '*Eileh*—These, Yisrael, are your gods.'"[6] It is interesting that the singular *eigel*, calf, is referred to in the plural as *eileh*, these. The *Sefas Emes* explains that the plural *eileh* represents the essence of *avodah zarah*. The first verse of the *Shema* serves as our proclamation of the most basic of our beliefs: "Hear, Yisrael: Hashem is our G-d, Hashem is One."[7] The idea of *Hashem Echad* is that there is One G-d and that everything that exists is a function of His Will. The idolatry of the *Eigel* is referred to as the plural *eileh* in that it represents one of the many different powers that serve as the underlying point for the falsehood called *avodah zarah*. All that relates to Hashem is anchored in terms of the recognition of Him as the One and Only. It is this point that is implied in the word *zos*.

Sefarim explain that *zos* represents the spiritual *pnim*, internal dimension, of all that exists in Hashem's world. Hashem is the One and Only; therefore, everything **must** contain the *Ratzon* of Hashem in order for it to be. The essence of all that is part of the world is that it in some way portrays the *Malchus*, Kingship, of Hashem. It is referred to as *zos*, this, because the special element that defines the true sense of being of everything is referred to as "this." The word "this" refers to the object, and all things are defined by the spiritual nature of their *pnim*. Therefore, the *pasuk* says: "*V'zos*...—And this is what their father spoke to them when he blessed them."

It was to Yaakov Avinu that the words of *Shema* were originally said. The *Shevatim* wished to assure their father that they, too, recognized that Hashem is the One and Only. The *shoresh*, or headquarters, for the revelation of the Oneness of Hashem is in Yaakov. The stones in *Parashas Vayeitzei* became one to serve the *tzaddik* Yaakov. He returned for the small jars in *Parashas Vayishlach* because he realized everything exists to serve Hashem, even small jars. Yaakov revealed the secret of *zos* to his children and blessed them. It is this *yesod* that is referred to in the *pasuk* of "*Zos chanukas ha'Mizbei'ach*."

---

6 *Shemos* 32:4.

7 *Devarim* 6:4.

The *Sefas Emes* explains that *Zos Chanukah* represents the sense that the eighth day is a culmination of the *kedushah* that is inherent in the Yom Tov of Chanukah. There is a profound idea from the *Maharal* that may add to our understanding of the *yesod* the *Sefas Emes* is teaching us.

Beis Shammai holds that the lighting of the *neiros Chanukah* should be in descending order, from eight on the first night, seven on the second night, until one on the eighth night. The *Maharal* explains that the opinion of *Beis Shammai* is based upon the idea that the first night of Chanukah serves as a sense of *reishis* and foundation for all of the *kedushah* that will eventually develop. Thus, on the first night, we light eight because in that night is included all eight days.

Beis Hillel, however, holds that "*maalin b'kodesh*," we go up in *kedushah*. Human beings require a process of development to eventually be able to relate to higher levels of holiness. Therefore, although the first night spiritually includes all eight days, *Beis Hillel* holds that our actual lighting of the *neiros* should be a reflection of our *avodah* on this Yom Tov. We light one *ner* to represent the beginning of **our** development in perceiving the *kedushah* of Chanukah. Chanukah teaches us that the physical world is derived and connected to its spiritual source, whereby, according to the *Maharal*, the world of *teva*, of "seven," comes from the world of pure spirituality, of "eight." According to *Beis Hillel*, only after the first seven days of Chanukah can the person recognize that the seven days of *teva* were born from the eighth day. To appreciate that there is something hidden, our fascination with the external and superficial has to be first deflated. People live their lives in search of true meaning, for they sense from deep within themselves that the superficial world just doesn't provide them with true meaning for their existence.

It is interesting that Hashem didn't create *kedushah* first; first the six mundane days of the week came into being, and only then did Shabbos, as the seventh day, become a reality. The emptiness of the physical world must first be experienced in order to recognize that there is something more—something beyond what appears before our eyes. This is why the eighth day is called *Zos Chanukah*, because on that day we are finally able to appreciate the true *pnim* of all things, that they exist to portray the *Malchus* of Hashem. Yaakov taught his children the lesson of *zos* and, on the eighth day, Klal Yisrael is able to recognize the *zos* of Chanukah—as well as the *zos* of all of Hashem's *briah.* For in our recognition of Hashem lies the true essence of the world and of ourselves, the ultimate *zos*.

Conclusion

THE WORLD WE live in is indeed a complicated one. We are in *galus*, and our ability to perceive the Presence of Hashem in the world as well as in our lives is something that we must constantly strive for. Within the darkness and suffering that Klal Yisrael has been subjected to, we pray for salvation. There was a person many years ago who was forced to live in a world of darkness, and it was through her that the *geulah* from Haman and Amalek ultimately took place. In a sense, she established the process for us to *emerge* from our state of darkness to that of light.

What was so special about Esther that she was chosen to be the *go'el*, redeemer?

The *Maharal* in *Ohr Chadash* discusses three points that serve to reveal the spiritual greatness of Esther and, as a result, why she was chosen to be the messenger to bring salvation to B'nei Yisrael in the *geulah* of Purim. One involves her name, one her family status, and one reveals her ability to be a true and valid messenger to serve as Hashem's vehicle for salvation.

Esther's name implies a sense of something hidden, as the *pasuk* in *Parashas Vayeilech* says: "*V'anochi haster astir*—I will surely have hidden My face."[1] Esther was also known by the name Hadassah, which reflects a similar idea. The Gemara describes the *hadas*, myrtle leaf, used as one of the Four Species on Sukkos, as something that its leaves cover and

1 Ibid., 31:18.

hide its stem. Esther is therefore defined as one who, in the midst of *hastaras panim*, when Hashem's Presence in His world was hidden, was able to see beyond the superficial and tap into the Presence of Hashem concealed within. We can appreciate this point from the words of the megillah, when Esther came before King Achashveirosh to plead for the lives of her people. The *pasuk* says: "Now it came to pass on the third day, Esther donned royalty and stood in the **inner** courtyard of the *beis ha'melech*—king's palace."[2] Later, when Haman comes to King Achashveirosh with his plan to hang Mordechai, the *pasuk* says: "Haman was coming into the **outer** courtyard of the *beis ha'melech*."[3] Chazal reveal that the word *melech*, king, when it appears in the megillah without the name of Achashveirosh, refers to Hashem as well. Thus, the *pasuk* relates the connection of Esther in terms of reaching a sense of internal relationship with Hashem, while Haman exists purely in terms of an external association—existing merely in the physical world. Chazal reveal that Esther was a *tzanuah*, one who is exceedingly modest and recognizes that the external physical world should not be paramount, that it is the internal, spiritual realm that bears the sense of *kedushah* and the true Presence of Hashem. Haman's world was purely the physical realm, and as such, he dwelled in the superficial world of the external depicted in the *pasuk*.

The *Maharal* explains how Esther's family status also played a role in her being chosen as Hashem's messenger. The *pasuk* in the megillah states: "And he [Mordechai] had reared Hadassah, she is Esther, his uncle's daughter, for she had neither father nor mother."[4] Esther was an orphan and was brought up by Mordechai. The state that Esther personally existed in—of having no parents and, in a sense, being all alone—reflected the status B'nei Yisrael were subject to in terms of their relationship with Hashem. Just as Esther had no parents to rely on—she was all alone and needed help and found it in Hashem—so too, B'nei Yisrael could not rely on anyone and were forced to develop

---

2 *Esther* 5:1.

3 Ibid., 6:4.

4 Ibid., 2:7.

their *emunah* and *bitachon* to pray for Hashem's help. Esther wasn't privy to the classical help we all rely on; she had to lean on Hashem, and this was the state of B'nei Yisrael as well. They could not rely on allies or members of government to help them; all they could hope for was the salvation of Hashem. Through Esther's high level of *bitachon*, B'nei Yisrael, too, were able to develop their belief in Hashem, do *teshuvah*, and pray for a *yeshuah*.

It was Esther's ability to serve as a proper messenger that enabled her to be chosen to serve as the *shaliach* of Hashem as well. The Mishnah in *Pirkei Avos* says: "Whoever repeats something in the name of the one who said it brings redemption to the world, as it is said, 'And Esther said to the king in the name of Mordechai.'"[5] We would assume that if B'nei Yisrael were worthy of salvation, the fact that Esther informed Achashveirosh of the threat of Bigsan and Seresh in the name of Mordechai was commendable and proper—but irrelevant. Yet, the *Maharal* explains that this served as the pivotal point in bringing salvation and Esther being chosen to be the redeemer.

Any *tzarah*, tragic situation, that Klal Yisrael is meant to endure serves a purpose in terms of the spiritual stature of B'nei Yisrael. The trials and tribulations are meant to cleanse them from where they have strayed from Hashem. But there exists an additional requirement that must be present in order for Hashem to bring them salvation and a *yeshuah* from their *tzarah*. They must realize that the source of their salvation is absolutely Hashem. Then their suffering has meaning in that it brings them to the clarity that reinforces their *emunah* and *bitachon* in the Creator. The *Maharal* says that Hashem would not bring salvation to B'nei Yisrael if they will not subsequently come to realize that it was indeed Him that brought it. Thus, had Esther chosen to take the credit for saving Achashveirosh instead of admitting that it was through Mordechai, she could never have been the vehicle of Hashem to save B'nei Yisrael from Haman. As the queen, it might have been theoretically assumed that her people were saved as a result of her power and influence. But by

---

5 6:6.

giving credit to Mordechai, she ultimately became worthy of serving as Hashem's *shaliach,* for, through her, Hashem would be recognized as the true Savior of B'nei Yisrael. This is why the Mishnah reveals that if one repeats something in the name of the one who originally said it, he brings redemption to the world.

Therefore, Esther was the ideal candidate for the role she played. She spiritually related to the hidden realm of *kedushah* in a time when all was dark, and the *yeshuah* had to come from that exalted Divine dimension. She knew that the *yeshuah* could only come from Hashem; a realization she had come to as an orphan growing up with no father and mother. She realized that when the salvation does occur, the true Source must be recognized as Hashem. It was through these three points that she was worthy of becoming Esther HaMalkah and serving as the *shaliach* to save Klal Yisrael. So too, recent events in world history are placing all in the position of Esther.

We have come to realize that what the secular world considers as substantial is nothing but an empty shell. We have been left as orphans, physically and spiritually, with our longing gaze now focusing on Hashem to bring our *yeshuah*. The lessons of life have brought us to the recognition that there is no one who really cares about us, and we can only rely on Hashem. We have matured and moved beyond the *sheker* of our world, to realize that the Only One Who can bring the ultimate *geulah* is Hashem. The miracle of Purim brought a *yeshuah* out of a state of darkness, while the *neis* of Chanukah turned darkness into light. We sincerely yearn to possess these *keilim* of redemption that will enable us to emerge from the darkness we are in so we can enter the *ohr* and light of the world of *geulah*.

Amen kein yehi ratzon.

About the Author

RABBI AHRON RAPPS, the *rosh yeshiva* of Yeshiva Zichron Shraga in Brooklyn, NY, is a *talmid* of Mesivta Yeshiva Rabbi Chaim Berlin and of Rav Moshe Shapiro, *zt"l*. He writes articles on *divrei machshavah* in *Yated Neeman* and has been giving *shiurim* on those *inyanim* in many venues, as well as having been a *madrich* to his many *talmidim* over the years. He is the *rav* of Kahal Shaarei Tefillah of Blue Ridge in Waterbury, CT.

לזכר נשמת

משה בן **אלעזר**

חדוה פריידל בת **אברהם דוד**

חיים משה אריה אלטער בן **דוב**

רחל לאה בת **אליהו שרגא**

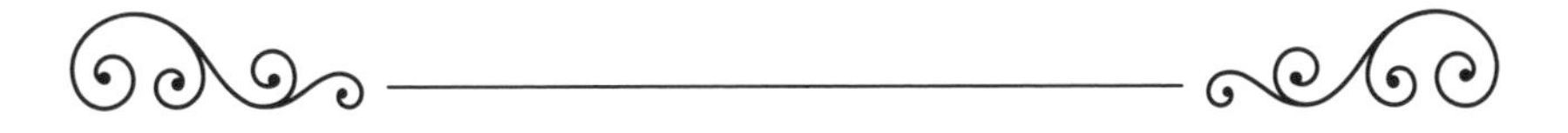

לעילוי נשמת

שיינא בת ר' **ראובן** ע"ה

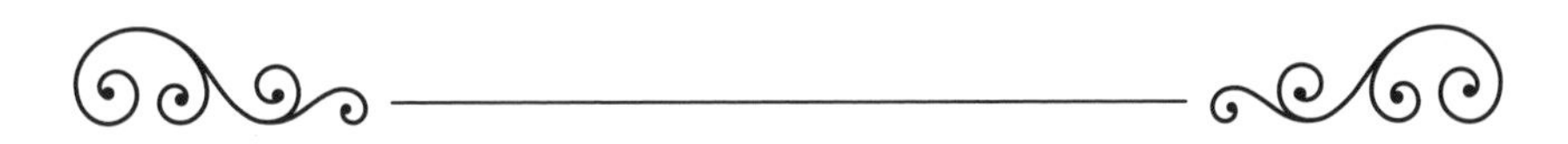

לעילוי נשמת

ר' אברהם בן יהודה ז"ל
רבקה בת ר' יוסף הכהן ע"ה
אייכהרן

MOISHE AND TOVA EICHHORN

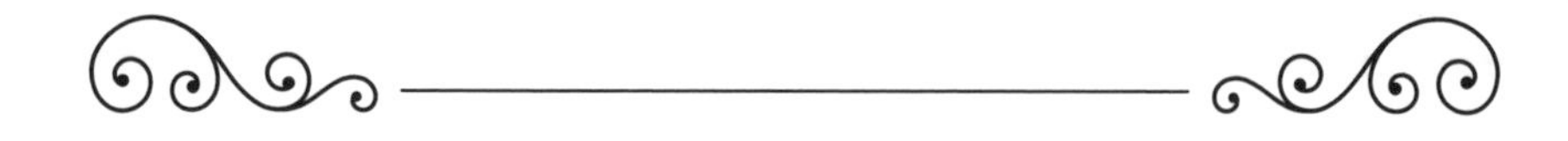

לזכר נשמת

הרב משה יוסף נחמיה
בן הרה"ג רב מנחם צבי אייזנשטאט

AKIVA AND AVIGAIL EISENSTADT

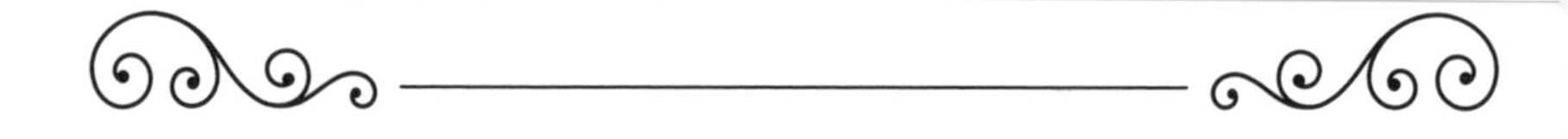